The Marys of the Bible

The Marys of the Bible

The Original #MeToo Movement

BOAZ JOHNSON

With Forewords
by INGRID FARO,
BINDULATA BARIK,
and ELIZABETH PIERRE

WIPF & STOCK · Eugene, Oregon

THE MARYS OF THE BIBLE
The Original #MeToo Movement

Wipf & Stock
An Imprint of Wipf and Stock Publishers
199 W. 8th Ave., Suite 3
Eugene, OR 97401

www.wipfandstock.com

PAPERBACK ISBN: 978-1-5326-5936-2
HARDCOVER ISBN: 978-1-5326-5937-9
EBOOK ISBN: 978-1-5326-5938-6

Manufactured in the U.S.A.   10/24/18

To my wife, Sarita, an amazing Eshet Chayil,
who taught me to care for the Marys of the world.

To my daughters, Karuna, Ruhi, Neena, and Allie,
who have themselves become strong women.

To my grand-daughters, Deborah, Hannah, and Abigail,
that they may become strong women.

Contents

Foreword

Dr. Ingrid Faro

Dean of Academic Affairs & Associate Professor of Old Testament
at Northern Seminary

It's impossible to know Boaz Johnson without knowing his heart for the hurting, the broken, and the abused. In his book, *The Marys of the Bible*, Boaz draws heavily from his background growing up in a New Delhi slum observing the injustices mainly against girls and women. These reflections, along with his deep faith, fueled his commitment to helping victims of human trafficking throughout the world, and the writing of this current book.

As he expresses so well, the Bible and the God of the Bible is often maligned as being against women but a close read of the Scriptures reveals an entirely different story. Rather, the story line demonstrates that God and those who follow God are counter-cultural to the patriarchal systems that subjugate women and girls as subservient to men. *The Marys of the Bible* points to specific women who had been put down and nearly cast aside but because of their bold faith in God and willingness to stand against their societal power structures are elevated in status and honor in Scripture.

Nevertheless, Scriptures have often been twisted to empower male dominance and enable exploitation and manipulation of others.

In my own life, the abuse that takes place in the church, by pastors, and by those who identify as Christians, became a personal matter.

The church network I was part of in my early 20's had groomed me well. Women were to be quiet in the church and our value as a woman was measured by being a good wife. Higher education for women was considered a waste of time and money. I was already a bit of a rebel, since I had completed college and then a Masters in Associated Medical Sciences (Nutrition and Public Health). I had conducted the research for my thesis in Israel. It was a successful and fabulous time there, which would help change my life again 20 years later.

But, when I returned home after nearly a year in Israel, I fell right back into the same church culture I had left. Before long I was engaged to Gary, whom I had known for many years. He was being trained to be a pastor by our pastor. Although I served on a committee at the American Dietetic Association, worked in community programs, directed county-wide nutrition programs, and eventually served as associated professor of nutrition at a state university, in the church my only value could be as a good wife. The highest value was to become a good pastor's wife. Gary was leading Bible studies, local evangelistic crusades, and had a third of the New Testament memorized. He could give a three-point sermon with ease and was well respected in the church. We set the date for our wedding. One month before our wedding he forced himself on me in my apartment. From then on I felt trapped, for now I thought I was used goods and convinced no one else could ever want me. Then two weeks before our wedding, he admitted to cheating on me and kicked me. Rather than being angry and breaking off our marriage, I was scared and silent. I believed that I had no choice but to go ahead with the marriage as a submissive wife. And, surely, if I tried hard enough, we would grow to love each other. Soon after marriage, we started in seminary together, taking Greek and Hebrew. The plan was for me to support him in his studies. However, he was mad that I did better than he did. So we quit.

Over the years, the abuse escalated from threats, holes in the wall and throwing objects to direct physical violence. He was angry that he wasn't more successful, that he wasn't making more money, and that his mother wasn't healed of her disease. He moved from working two jobs, to one, to none. He began going out late at night, drinking regularly and eventually frequenting strip clubs. Occasionally, I would drive around to find him to bring him home. I did all I could to try to make him happy. Of course, nothing helped. Later he would complain that I was "too nice." Meanwhile, I began working two jobs to pay off the signature loans he had taken out and to cover his spending.

The threats and bruises increased, but I would cover them up and make excuses for them. Until he swung and broke my nose while I was driving us to visit my parents for Christmas. I pulled over, dizzy and bleeding profusely. When I caught my breath I drove him home, and myself to the ER. The surgeon urged me to file a report. I denied physical violence, until he said, "Look, I can see the imprint of a ring on your nose! At least promise me you won't go home." After leaving the ER, I drove myself to a hotel, and there called our Pastor. After telling him for the first time of the physical violence, his only response was, "Go home and love your husband." I hung up, and drove home.

Of course, the abuse and violence escalated. I continued working my two jobs, one in my career and a weekend and evening job in insurance to make some extra money. We held all our accounts together. Large amounts would disappear. I kept working and said nothing. Sometimes I was locked out of the house if I came home late from work, and then slept in my car. Only my sister knew what was going on, not because I told her, but only because she had been through it herself. But I admitted nothing to anyone. My sister asked me once, "Are you happy?" and I replied, "What does that have to do with life!" And that conversation was over.

Until one afternoon, Gary started yelling at me again, shoved me down, and pinned me on the bed, his legs on mine, and his forearm pressed upon my throat. I couldn't move. I pleaded until I could no longer breathe. I looked into his eyes and all I saw were black holes. I later learned that this is called "shark eyes." Although he was staring at me, there was no one home. I closed my eyes and said silently, "Lord, into Your hands I commend my spirit." I wanted to go home. I was ready to die. I had tremendous peace. I remember no pain.

As I lay there in the silence, the doorbell rang. It was sharp. Piercing! I opened my eyes and saw my husband lift up his head, then release me, get off the bed and go to the door. His movements seemed mechanical. It was surreal. He was gone for a bit. I was able to stand up, confused, and in fact, disappointed that I was still alive. Then I heard a clear voice speaking within me, quoting Psalm 118, "You shall not die, but live, and declare My glory." This was followed by, "But if you stay, you will die." It took me six months to plan my escape since I was followed and tracked. I managed to stay alive, began going to counseling, and reached out to a friend and to my sister. The healing began. Eventually, I escaped to a safe place and began the long healing process. Gary admitted to infidelity, but never admitted to the abuse. Thankfully we had no children. We divorced, and for years I thought I was disqualified from any ministry. For a long time, I couldn't face going to church and God's love was just a theological construct. I threw myself into my business. I remarried and we had a son – but it took many years for the trauma to heal. Some years into my second marriage, Gary died in a hit and run accident, and I finally stopped looking over my shoulder to see if I was being followed.

Most victims of abuse have been selected and groomed. Abuse often begins with small manipulations and coercions. Abuse always escalates unless it's stopped early on. Abusers will not change unless there are direct, harsh, enforceable consequences for their behavior. And then, only a very small percent ever change. What we permit we promote. What are we permitting in our churches?

Statistics from the National Coalition Against Domestic Violence (2015)

- 1 in 5 women and 1 in 59 men in the United States is raped during his/her lifetime.

- 1 in 3 women and 1 in 4 men have been physically abused by an intimate partner.

- 1 in 5 women and 1 in 7 men have been severely physically abused by an intimate partner.

- 1 in 3 female murder victims and 1 in 20 male murder victims are killed by intimate partners.

Eventually, the Lord led me to go to seminary to seek answers about evil and abuse from the Bible for myself, in the Greek and the Hebrew. After years of study and searching I came to discover the love of God as a tangible reality. I learned that love in the Old Testament means a covenant commitment to the well-being of another. God has this kind of love towards us, and wants people to love, and treat, one another in that way. From the New Testament I learned that "agape" means to highly value, to greatly esteem. God so highly values and greatly esteems each one of us that He laid down His life to redeem us to Himself, and calls us to do likewise for one another. Any system or form of Christianity that does not exemplify this kind of love is giving a perverted perspective of God.

In *The Marys of the Bible,* Boaz seeks to demonstrate *this* God, *this* Jesus Christ, to those who have misjudged God due to those who have misrepresented Him and the Bible. I pray many will find healing through the journey of reading this book.

Foreword

Bindulata Barik

Chair, Taskforce on Women's Abuse and Domestic Violence, Evangelical Fellowship
of India, New Delhi, India

Ph.D. candidate, SHUATS University, Allahabad, India.

I am both stunned and invigorated after reading this book manuscript. I thank Prof. Boaz Johnson, my professor, from the bottom of my heart for letting me read the pre-publication draft of his book, *The Marys of the Bible: The Original #MeToo Movement*. The name of the book tells it all. Through this book he has mentored me in a very deep and personal way. The reading of this manuscript has been a healing experience for me. It challenges me and makes me more responsible to understand and present the Word of God in its original context. It will definitely bring healing to victims like me; and it will challenge people to understand the gravity of women's abuse, throughout history and today.

A birth of a girl child is not celebrated in India, where I was reared. It was not celebrated in the history of humanity. Girls have always been considered to be merely sex objects. In India, there are many myths that surround the birth of a girl-her virginity and marriage. Reading this book has made me realize that this was true in Ancient Near Eastern civilizations, as well. There are many traditions, in India, of marrying virgin girls with divine trees, animals, gods, and goddess. Girls are forced to have their first sexual experience with a priest, and other high caste or powerful men in the community before their marriage, all in the name of religious rituals. Prof. Boaz Johnson shows in this book that these abuses of women were seen in ancient religions as well, and that the Bible is the original #MeToo movement. He brings to this a rich background research in Ancient Near Eastern literature.

I am a survivor of child sexual abuse. It happened so early in my life. I don't remember who first violated me, or when did this first happen. However, I distinctly remember the abuse. I was 3 years old. Different men abused me over a period of time since then. I did not understand it as evil. I accepted it as a normal behaviour. I never complained or reported about it to anyone. When I realized that it was evil, it was too late. When I was a teenager, a man tried to force himself upon me. I somehow picked up the courage to protect myself. Yet even then, I couldn't complain to anyone. I had not dealt with my past wounds. These had made me numb and vulnerable. I remained silent. The social taboos related to the loss of virginity had damaged my inner being. I was frustrated and tried to commit suicide three times, but I failed. I felt guilty, because of my inability to report my sexual abuse, and my suicidal attempts.

I had become a Christian by then, and I prayed constantly. I thanked God for protecting my life. I reflected on the Lord's Prayer, and sought to forgive the men who sinned against me. He taught me to forgive those persons who had sinned against me, so that my sins could be forgiven. I received assurance that my sins have been removed as far as the east is from the west (Psalm 13:12). However, I did not talk about my abuse with anyone. It remained buried in my heart.

I am a Christian leader now. After about fifty years of this hidden secret, I began working with an organization which sought to address issues of violence against women in India. I began work on a project entitled "Ending Domestic Violence: What can the Church do?" During work on this project, in a fresh way, God spoke to me. I came to realize the victims of abuse, like me, need to speak up boldly against the perpetrators. The power is in our hands. Not in their hands. It suddenly struck me that I was living a fake life, wearing a mask. I realized that shame and fear were still controlling me, and the mighty acts of God in my life could not bear fruit.

During my PhD studies at SHUATS university, I shared with Prof. Boaz Johnson this hidden pain. He counselled me, and promised that he will write a biblical theological engagement with issues of women's abuse. As I read this book, it has been a therapeutic experience to deal with my wounds of sexual abuse. It has given me clarity from a biblical perspective. I realized that it's not #Me alone. I came to realize that from first woman,

Eve, women and girls have been victimized and have lived vulnerable lives. So, now I join this ancient #MeToo movement- the women of the Bible!

Some worldviews legitimize sexual abuse of girls and women. I was a victim of such a worldview. Sadly, the Church in India has also absorbed this worldview. The influence of neighbouring religions and culture leads to a misunderstanding of the Word of God. In this book Prof. Boaz Johnson has clarified many of these misunderstandings, and has interpreted the Hebrew and Greek text, with a detailed background study of the context. He proves that the Bible in fact counters the neighbouring abusive worldviews. The God of the Bible hears the #MeToo cries of women. He rescues and heals the victims of abuse, and restores the dignity of women. He does this by restoring their original identity as His image bearers and co-creators. He does this even today.

He has restored #MeToo. He has transformed me from a victim to survivor. I am now a care giver to victims of abuse. He made me co-creator with him. Many victims of sexual abuse are been healed and restored through my testimony.

So, I dare to say #MeToo!

Like me, I now want the victims of abuse to know that they have not sinned. They are victims. I want them to know that they have the ability to fight for their rights, and can restore their dignity. I want the Church to know that the victims should not be blamed, but rather be rescued and restored. Women are not sexual objects. Women are not merely the bearers of children. Women are image bearers of God. Women are co-creators with him. The Virgin Mary is the bearer of God. Through Mary, God sent his Son to restore the fallen world. He transformed the bitter lives of the Marys (women of the Bible) to be the Blessed ones.

This book and I invite Christian men to join the #MeToo movement. Whenever men in the Bible stood alongside the #MeToo movement, it restored the dignity and worth of victims of abuse.

I strongly believe that reading this book will heal the victims, discipline the perpetrators, and strengthen the caregivers. I believe it will bring an end to sexual abuse, and the concomitant culture of silence. The modern #MeToo movement challenges the church to face this evil. The biblical #MeToo movement rescues and heals women, and restores the original dignity of women.

Foreword

Dr. Elizabeth Pierre

Dr. Elizabeth Pierre is Assistant Professor of Pastoral Counseling at North Park Theological Seminar, Chicago, Illinois, USA. She teaches graduate courses in the Seminary and the School of Professional Studies. In her academic and clinical counselling work she specializes in the trauma care of girls and women who are victims of emotional, physical, and sexual abuse.

As a professor who teaches and researches the intersection between trauma and faith, what exacerbates the impact of trauma for survivors of sexual abuse is the minimization or lack of acknowledgement of the experience. Sadly, this has been the case for many in our communities of faith.

Rachael Denhollander, a Christian and one of the many young girls sexually abused by Olympic physician, Larry Nassar, says the following about how the Christians ought to respond to survivors:

> But she hopes Christians and others hear both sides of her message: The gospel is glorious and forgiveness is possible, but God is also concerned with justice. They are "both Biblical pursuits and both can be pursued simultaneously."
>
> She hopes churches will face the importance of reporting abuse allegations to civil authorities ordained by God to handle criminal acts. And she hopes they'll learn more about how to help victims confront the trauma abuse brings—not just encourage them to move on from it.
>
> Jacob (her husband) says when he looked out over the courtroom, he longed to see churches reaching out to women craving justice and help to cope with the sorrows they've endured: "This

is a mission field ripe for the taking if we can speak to these." He longs to see "an army of women healed by the gospel."[1]

Essentially, what Rachael (along with the many voices of the #MeToo movement) is calling her fellow believers to do is bear witness to the suffering of so many women who have been victims of sexual assault. Such a witness empathizes and seeks a way to bring both justice and to alleviate further pain.

Dr. Boaz Johnson's book serves as such a witness to the Marys in the Bible and to the myriad of Marys in the world who are crying out for their voices to be heard and for others to journey with them in their suffering and their journey toward hope in Jesus Christ. It's not any easy journey. However, Dr. Johnson's book engages journey critically, theologically, and with great compassion. It's a must read within churches and academic settings to learn how to thoughtfully minister to those who have experienced such sexual violence.

1. https://world.wng.org/2018/03/a_time_to_speak

Introduction

I have recently returned from a trip to the largest refugee camp in the world—the Kakuma Refugee Camp in Kenya. In this desert, among the Turkana people, there are more than 180,000 people cramped together in a sprawling shanty town complex run by the UNHCR, the United Nations Refugee Agency. I went there with a delegation of the The Evangelical Covenant Church, USA. We landed at Nairobi Airport, and then flew to Kakuma on a special UN flight.

The stories and sights of the Kakuma refugee camp will be forever etched my mind. I met girls and boys who saw their whole family killed in front of their little eyes. They somehow escaped and walked for months together in the wilderness from places like South Sudan, Congo, and Somalia, to get to Kakuma. We heard stories from girls who were gang raped by an enemy tribe's militia. We heard stories of thirteen-year-old girls being sold by their uncles to some eighty-year-old men so they could receive cattle in exchange. Bright young girls in this sprawling camp do not see any hope. The civil wars continue to go on for years without any end in sight. Women told our delegation, "We are burying our people in this refugee camp. We do not want to die here. We want to die in our own country."

I went to Africa with a delegation from the Covenant World Relief Board. From Kakuma Refugee Camp we went to Nairobi, Kenya, and met with Congolese refugees who have fled the civil war in the Democratic Republic of Congo (DRC). They somehow were able to find some life outside the Kakuma Refugee Camp. But the Kenyans around them do not want them. They are treated as scum.

From Nairobi, we went to Goma, in the DRC. There we heard horrible stories of thirteen- to fifteen-year-old girls being raped by opposing militia who control large sections of the DRC. Rape is a method of war and control. When these girls get pregnant, they are thrown out by their own families, because they are carrying the babies of enemy militia.

I was reared in a New Delhi slum. Slums in much of the world are places where you see much sadness and injustice. Much of these injustices are promulgated against girls, boys, and women, though mainly girls and women. Many of these boys and girls are taken into sexual slavery when they are ten to fifteen years old. Many girls and boys become slaves in the garment, brick, or carpet industries. Newspapers in India are, even today, replete with stories of this kind.

A March 7, 2017 Reuters News report stated that,

> Almost 20,000 women and children were victims of human trafficking in India in 2016, a rise of nearly 25 percent from the previous year, government data released on Thursday showed. The Ministry of Women and Child Development told parliament that 19,223 women and children were trafficked last year against 15,448 in 2015, with the highest number of victims recorded in the eastern state of West Bengal . . . The official said the actual figure could be much higher as many victims were still not registering cases with the police, largely because they did not know the law or feared traffickers. South Asia, with India at its center, is one of the fastest-growing regions for human trafficking in the world. Thousands of people—largely poor, rural women and children—are lured to India's towns and cities each year by traffickers who promise good jobs, but sell them into modern day slavery. Some end up as domestic workers, or forced to work in small industries such as textile workshops, farming or are even pushed into brothels where they are sexually exploited. In many cases, they are not paid or are held in debt bondage. Some go missing, and their families cannot trace them . . . The desert state of Rajasthan recorded the second highest number of trafficked children in 2016, while the western state of Maharashtra, where India's business capital Mumbai is located, showed the second highest number of trafficked women.[1]

I am on the Board of Covenant World Relief, an arm of the Evangelical Covenant Church. In our meetings, we discuss the works of organizations which are addressing issues related to a range of evils across the world. Human trafficking of children and women is at the top of the list.

One organization with which we work is called Covenant Social Services. This is an arm of the Hindustani Covenant Church in India. This

---

1. Bhalla, "Almost 20,000 Women and Children," paras. 1–2, 6–10, 14.

amazing organization rescues many women in the western state of Maharashtra who have become trapped in the web of injustice which enslaves minor boys and girls in the sex industry. The International Justice Mission, similarly, squarely takes on this business of sexual violence and rescues girls in different parts of the world such as India, Cambodia, and Thailand. They estimate that 2 million girls are enslaved in this industry. Human trafficking is a $150 billion-a-year industry. Two-thirds of this income is from the sexual exploitation of girls.

Why are human trafficking and sex trafficking so common in these countries? It seems clear to me that the common undergirding cause is the caste system so prevalent in Hinduism and Hindu-influenced countries.

I saw the impact of this in the slum where I was reared. Life in the slum was not easy. My neighbors belonged to the lowest castes and the outcasts of society. They were either the low-castes, the Shudras—the *dhobis*, the *bhangis*, the *chamars*—or they were outcasts. Gandhi called them *Harijan*, or "God's people," but no one treated them like God's people. They were treated like dirt. The slum was outside a major hospital. The doctors, the nurses, and regular high-caste people would walk at a distance from us. They belonged to the high-castes of society such as the *Brahmins* (the priests), the *Kshatriyas* (the militaristic caste), or the *Vyashiyas* (the business caste). My people, my neighbors, cleaned the latrines for these people. They washed their dirty clothes. They served in their houses, doing dirty tasks. But my people were never allowed to sit with these people. The only luxury the men enjoyed was the *hookah*, the tobacco-smoking pipe, when it was really dark. This was the tobacco that took away their lives, oh so early!

It would have been okay if life were just the way it was. Unfortunately, I saw kids disappear. They disappeared because their parents were poor and needed to borrow money from the high-caste moneylenders. They were poor because the high-castes charged them enormous amounts of money for common things like birth, sickness, marriage, and death. They were poor because the high-caste politicians charged them enormous amounts of money just to do common things like get a ration card to buy a little food.

Most families were in enormous debt, so they had to give their sons to the *bania* caste people, the businessmen. The *banias* would come to these families and say, "Don't worry, your children will live well," but the truth was just the opposite. Boys and girls—even my friends—were enslaved in the carpet, garment, and furniture industries. Pretty girls, as soon as they got their first menstrual cycle were taken to the brothels of Delhi, Mumbai, and Calcutta. Ironically, the red-light district into which these thirteen- and fourteen-year-old girls were taken was called Mahatma Gandhi Road.

THE RELIGIOUS DEMARCATION OF THE WEAK AND THE STRONG

There are several Hindu texts which make this kind of horrible practice the norm.

The Dalits are the untouchables of India, *atishudras*. The Hindu brahmanical texts define these people as lower than human beings. Dalit intellectuals have realized that the consciousness of their people was shaped by Vedic and puranic myths. It served the interests of the dominant castes and classes. A consciousness based on ancient history had to be formed to strengthen their existential identity.

The Vedas are the documents of Aryans that came into India around 1700–1400 BC, about the same time as the Hebrew people were enslaved by the Egyptians. They were lighter-skinned people from central Asia, and considered the original dwellers to be racially, socially, and mentally inferior. Their documents, called the *Vedas*—the *Rig Veda, Sama Veda, Yajur Veda*, and *Atharva Veda*—were the formative materials which dictated how they must understand themselves and how must they understand the racially inferior original dwellers of India. The latter were called the *Shudras* or slaves; and the *atishudras*, or the outcasts:

> When they divided the Purusha, into how many parts did they arrange him? What was his mouth? What were his arms? What are his thighs and feet called? The Brahmin, (the Priest) was his mouth, his arms were made the rajanya (warriors), his two thighs Vaishyas (traders and agriculturists), and from his feet the shudras (slave class) were born.[2]

Under the feet of this Aryan god-man, the *Purusha*, were the *atishudras*, the outcasts. Therefore, the low-castes that come from the feet of the *Purusha* and the outcasts, that come from under the feet of the *Purusha*, the Aryan god-man, are meant to be treated like dirt.

Manu Dharma Shastra is the main document which gives laws on what to do or not do with the *Shudras* and the *Atishudras*:

---

2. Griffith, *Rig Veda*, 5:603.

> But the Shudra, whether bought or unbought, he may compel to
> do the work of a slave; for he was created by the self-existent (svy-
> anbhu) to be the slave of the Brahmin.[3]

Based on these texts, the *Brahmins,* or priests, are the highest caste.
The *Kshatriyas* are the rulers. In later legends called the *Puranas,* the rulers
and the priests combine together. They are the Divine-kings. These are gods
like *Rama, Vishnu,* and *Krishna,* who are worshipped in popular Hindu
religion. The next category of people are the *Vyashiyas* or the *Banias.* These
are the businessmen. All three of these high-castes—the priests, rulers or
warriors, and the traders—descend from the Aryans. The images of their
gods and goddesses are always made from white marble, to depict their
racial superiority. The images of the low-caste people, the *Shudras* or slaves,
are always made with black marble.

The *Shudras* and the *Atishudras* were the original inhabitants of India.
The *Vedas* assert that these groups ought to be enslaved by the Aryans. Here
are a couple examples of treatment of *Shudras,* slaves from later legends:

> A Sudra should be deprived of his tongue if he abuses violently a
> twice-born, if his offence be moderate; if his offence be highest,
> he is to be fined Uttama Sahasa. A king should put a red-hot iron
> spike twelve Angulas long in the mouth of a Sudra who vilifies
> violently by taking his name, caste, or house. A Sudra who teaches
> Dharma to the twice-born should also be punished by a sovereign
> by getting hot oil poured into his ears and mouth. (Matsya Purana
> 227.73–75)
>
> A Kshatriya who abuses a Brahmana should be fined 100 Panas, a
> Vaisya doing so should be fined 200 Panas, and a Sudra if he does
> so should be sentenced to death. (Matsya Purana 227.67–68)
>
> Thenceforward all this world will fall upon very evil times (Kali-
> yuga). Men will be liars, greedy, and destitute of righteousness, af-
> fection and wealth. The religion of Srutis and Smritis will become
> nonexistent, and so also will be destroyed the orders and castes.
> The people will be of mixed origin, weak in body and will be led
> astray and deluded. Brahmanas will sacrifice for Sudras (or will
> study under Sudraas) and Sudras will take to teaching Mantras.
> (Matsya Purana 273.46–47)

Hindu texts are divided into two categories: The primary texts are
called the *Shruti* religious documents. These are documents like the *Vedas*

---

3. Bühler, *Laws of Manu,* 413–14.

and the *Upanishads*. The secondary texts are called the *Smriti*. These are religious legends like the *Ramayana*, and the *Mahabharata*. The *Shruti* set the philosophical grounding of the demarcation between the strong and the weak. The *Smriti* documents and legends reinforce the demarcation between the two.

In both sets of documents it becomes clear the strong are the three highest castes, and the weak are the *Shudras* and the *Dalits*.

THE RELIGIOUS DEMARCATION OF THE WOMEN—THE WEAKEST OF WEAK

According to Rigveda 1.48.3, Aryan Hinduism venerates trees like the *peepal* tree, and the *Nyagrodha*, fig tree. *Soma* is the god of plants, the fig plant. From this plant, girls from low-castes, the *Shudras*, are given the intoxicating drink before they participate in the religious sexual ritual. When high-caste gurus meditate under these trees, they experience divinity. According to the *Matsaya sutra*, before a low-caste girl marries a low-caste man, she must first have religiously oriented sex with a guru under these trees. Only then may they marry. Other girls would devote their lives to the worship of the *peepal* tree, and the god Vishnu who resides in the *peepal* tree. These girls are called *Devadasis*, or slave of the god, a Hindu form of sacred prostitution in the states of Karnataka and Tamil Nadu. In the state of Andhra Pradesh, they go by different names: *Jogins and Mathas*. These religious rituals form the basis of temple prostitution in India.

In a well-researched paper, Maggie Black makes the following comments

> Devadasis can be seen to suffer from a number of other gross violations of their human rights as laid down in other international treaties, including the 1989 Convention on the Rights of the Child. These include:
>
> - Girls are dedicated and initiated without their consent, and usually have no knowledge of what becoming a Jogin, Matha or Devadasi will involve;
>
> - They are not "free," in the sense that they become the servant of the deity and the common property of her devotees, and have no decision-making say over the nature and content of their lives;

- They are subject to gross exploitation, in the form of sexual servitude or nonconsensual sex with one or many partners, often on demand;

- They are prevented from marrying and leading a normal family life, nor can they enjoy the social standing of a wife and mother;

- They are denied protection from exploitation, discrimination, verbal abuse, and insults, from which their "holy" status does not shield them;

- They are unable to escape or renounce the cultural status of Jogini, Mathamma or Devadasi; the status follows them through life;

- Some give up their name to be known merely as Mathamma or Jogini, a breach of their right to a name and personal identity.[4]

Because of this religious sanction of rape culture in the Hindu religion, in recent times there have been many reports of Hindu gurus being arrested and convicted of rape. However, Indian journalists report that only a minute fraction of the god-men who are accused are then brought to justice.[5]

I have taken my students to India to engage with these deep issues of injustice against the weak and the marginalized—mostly girls and women. I have also taken students to other parts of the world, including South Africa, Congo, Mexico, and Brazil. I have found that the issues are very similar. It is always the weak and the marginalized—usually girls and women—who face gross injustice.

The questions I often ask myself and my students are, "Why is there so much evil in the world today? Why is it that it is always the weak and the vulnerable who suffer the most?" It is clear that this is the case in India and hundreds of other global situations, which one can see if only one cares to see.[6]

In his preface to the powerful classic, entitled *Our Contempt for Weakness: Nazi Norms and Values—and our Own*, Harald Ofstad, a Norwegian

---

4. Black, "Women in Ritual Slavery," 179–205.

5. See, for example, Dhillon, "Indian Judge Jails 'God Man.'"

6. See, for example, Maogi, "Turning Poverty Around"; Kippenberg, *Soldiers Who Rape*; Stiglmayer, *Mass Rape*; and Rittner and Roth, *Rape*.

moral philosopher, who taught at Stockholm University, made the following crucial observation:

> If we examine ourselves in the mirror of Nazism we see our own traits—enlarged but so revealing for that very reason. Anti-Semitism is not the essence of Nazism. Its essence is the doctrine that the "strong" shall rule over the "weak," and that the "weak" are contemptible because they are "weak." Nazism did not originate in the Germany of the nineteen thirties, and did not disappear in 1945. It expresses deeply rooted tendencies which are constantly alive in and around us. We admire those who fight their way to the top, and are contemptuous of the loser . . . We consider ourselves rid of Nazism because we abhor the gas chambers. We forget they were the ultimate product of a philosophy which despised the "weak" and admired the "strong." The brutal Nazism was not just the product of certain historical conditions in Germany. It was also the consequence of a certain philosophy of life, a given set of norms, values, perceptions and reality.[7]

My rearing in a New Delhi slum, my travels to lecture in different parts of the world—many times with my students from North Park University—and my engagement with Covenant World Relief partners, all of these things make it clear to me that Harald Ofstad is very right about this crucial observation. The weak, throughout the world and throughout history, have always been treated with contempt. Historically, the norms of society have been so designed that the weak become weaker and the strong become stronger. Norms of society have been so designed that the injustices of the strong against the weak have been made to look like justice. These observations can only lead one to more despair.

THE #METOO MOVEMENT

In the United States, almost every day there is an article on the #MeToo movement in prominent publications like the *New York Times* and *Time Magazine*. In 2006, a sexual assault survivor named Tarana Burke began the first "MeToo," on Myspace.[8] She did this to help girls and women of color heal from sexual violence. However, the #MeToo movement took deep and extensive traction after October 5, 2017, when the *New York Times* broke

---

7. Ofstad, *Our Contempt for Weakness*, 5.

8. See Garcia, "Woman Who Created #MeToo."

the story about Oscar-winning Hollywood producer Harvey Weinstein. The article begins with the following:

> Two decades ago, the Hollywood producer Harvey Weinstein invited Ashley Judd to the Peninsula Beverly Hills hotel for what the young actress expected to be a business breakfast meeting. Instead, he had her sent up to his room, where he appeared in a bathrobe and asked if he could give her a massage or she could watch him shower, she recalled in an interview.
>
> "How do I get out of the room as fast as possible without alienating Harvey Weinstein?" Ms. Judd said she remembers thinking.
>
> In 2014, Mr. Weinstein invited Emily Nestor, who had worked just one day as a temporary employee, to the same hotel and made another offer: If she accepted his sexual advances, he would boost her career, according to accounts she provided to colleagues who sent them to Weinstein Company executives. The following year, once again at the Peninsula, a female assistant said Mr. Weinstein badgered her into giving him a massage while he was naked, leaving her "crying and very distraught," wrote a colleague, Lauren O'Connor, in a searing memo asserting sexual harassment and other misconduct by their boss.
>
> "There is a toxic environment for women at this company," Ms. O'Connor said in the letter, addressed to several executives at the company run by Mr. Weinstein.[9]

On October 15, 2017, actor Alyssa Milano tweeted, "If all the women who have been sexually harassed or assaulted wrote 'Me too.' as a status, we might give people a sense of the magnitude of the problem." On October 24, 2017, Alyssa Milano tweeted, "One tweet has brought together 1.7 million voices from 85 countries. Standing side by side, together, our movement will only grow. #MeToo" At the same time, Facebook also stated that there were more that 12 million posts in connection with the #MeToo movement.

Millions of women from all over the world have responded to the #MeToo campaign. Many of these are from countries I have mentioned in the first part of this chapter, such as India, Kenya, Congo, and South Sudan, and many countries from the West have joined the #MeToo hashtag movement, including Germany, Italy, France, and Sweden. Other countries like Afghanistan, China, Israel, and Japan have also joined the movement.

9. Kantor and Twohey, "Harvey Weinstein Paid off Sexual Harassment Accusers for Decades," paras. 1–4.

In 2017, *Time Magazine* chose #MeToo as its Person of the Year. This remarkable issue detailed the horrible experiences of The Silence Breakers—actors and singers like Ashley Judd, Rose McGowan, Alyssa Milano, Selma Blair, and Taylor Swift. It went on to detail the awful stories of women seeking to do their regular jobs in all kinds of industries such as journalism, IT, and hotels. The men who were accused of sexual harassment are some of the most powerful and known men in the last two to three decades.

This is truly a global campaign, and rightly so because women and girls have been sexually harassed and violated all over the world.

As I review this manuscript, two cases have gained prominence: one in India, and the other in the US.

Women's groups in India have gained courage, thankfully, from the #MeToo movement. Something that once would have been unheard of is happening in different parts of India. On April 25, 2018, the *New York Times* reported, "An Indian court on Wednesday sentenced an influential guru to life in prison for the rape of a teenage girl, putting to rest a long legal battle that has been marred by the murder of at least two witnesses connected to the case." This sentence was handed to one of the most powerful god-men in India—Guru Asaram Bapu. His following includes some of the most powerful politicians, including the Prime Minister of India, several cabinet ministers, chief ministers, and businessmen. He has 400 ashrams around the world, and is known for his meditation and yoga techniques. According to his website, he has 40 million devotees across the world, primarily of Hindu origin.

In 2013, Guru Asaram Bapu gave a sixteen-year-old girl, who was his devotee, intoxicating potions and raped her while her parents stood outside chanting prayers to him. They trusted that he was delivering her of some evil powers.

It has also been reported that Asaram Bapu is on trial for rapes that he has committed on other girl devotees. The awful thing is that several witnesses to these crimes have been attacked and a couple of them have been killed.

In December 2012 a medical student in Delhi was gang-raped on a public transport bus. Women's groups and college students all over India came out in thousands to draw attention to this, and many other rapes. Yet, this same Hindu guru told his followers, "Guilt is not one-sided," adding that if the student had pleaded with her six attackers in God's name, and told them she was of the "weaker sex," they would have relented.[10]

This shows the immensity of the problem in India. It also shows that thousands of these kinds of crimes by god-men and high-caste people are not reported at all. God-men who rape in the name of religious sex do not get prosecuted.

In the USA, on April 26, 2018, actor and comedian Bill Cosby, the great father figure for two generations of people, was found guilty of drugging and sexually assaulting a woman. Ms. Andrea Constad, a Temple University employee, considered him to be a mentor. Ms. Constad is the only woman among more than fifty accusers whose case was brought to trial.

In many senses, this conviction is a victory for the #MeToo movement.

Nevertheless, it is clear that this is not a new evil—it has been happening for thousands of years, all over the world.

I am a biblical theologian. My PhD is in ancient Near Eastern languages and literature. I have done advanced studies in the Hebrew Bible. I have done much research in the ancient and modern religions of the world. That is what I teach. So, the obvious question I ask myself is, "Does the Bible have any answers to this horrible quandary?"

This is the question this book seeks to explore.

My thesis is the Bible is the original #MeToo movement.

It was a #MeToo movement in the context of the religions of society of the days when the Bible was written.

It was a #MeToo Movement that directly countered against perspectives of women that was very similar to the perspective of women I saw in the slum where I was reared.

It was a #MeToo movement that gave women a voice during that time.

It is a #MeToo movement which gives women a voice even today.

---

10. Daniel and Bhattacharjya, "Asaram Bapu's View," para. 3.

1

The #MeToo Movement in the Introduction to Matthew

THE GENEALOGY OF JESUS THE MESSIAH: THE THESIS STATEMENT OF THE NEW TESTAMENT

The New Testament opens with the following words,

This is the genealogy of Jesus the Messiah the son of David, the son of Abraham: Abraham was the father of Isaac, Isaac the father of Jacob, Jacob the father of Judah and his brothers, Judah the father of Perez and Zerah, whose mother was Tamar, Perez the father of Hezron, Hezron the father of Ram, Ram the father of Amminadab, Amminadab the father of Nahshon, Nahshon the father of Salmon, Salmon the father of Boaz, whose mother was Rahab, Boaz the father of Obed, whose mother was Ruth, Obed the father of Jesse, and Jesse the father of King David. David was the father of Solomon, whose mother had been Uriah's wife, Solomon the father of Rehoboam, Rehoboam the father of Abijah, Abijah the father of Asa, Asa the father of Jehoshaphat, Jehoshaphat the father of Jehoram, Jehoram the father of Uzziah, Uzziah the father of Jotham, Jotham the father of Ahaz, Ahaz the father of Hezekiah, Hezekiah the father of Manasseh, Manasseh the father of Amon, Amon the father of Josiah, and Josiah the father of Jeconiah and his brothers at the time of the exile to Babylon. After the exile to Babylon: Jeconiah was the father of Shealtiel, Shealtiel the father of Zerubbabel, Zerubbabel the father of Abihud, Abihud the father of Eliakim, Eliakim the father of Azor, Azor the father of Zadok,

Zadok the father of Akim, Akim the father of Elihud, Elihud the father of Eleazar, Eleazar the father of Matthan, Matthan the father of Jacob, and Jacob the father of Joseph, the husband of Mary, and Mary was the mother of Jesus who is called the Messiah. Thus, there were fourteen generations in all from Abraham to David, fourteen from David to the exile to Babylon, and fourteen from the exile to the Messiah. (Matt 1:1–17 NIV)

This introduction sets the groundwork for the mission of the gospel, the good news of Jesus the Messiah. On the surface, this seems like a very mundane reading of the names of all the people in the genealogy of Jesus the Messiah. It begins with Abraham and ends with Joseph, the earthly father of Jesus. It divides up the history of the Old Testament into three parts. Each part has fourteen generations (Matt 1:17). The first generation is from Abraham till the time of the beginning of the Davidic dynasty (Matt 1:2–6a). The second part is from the kingship of David till the Babylonian exile (Matt 1:6b–11). The third section is from the Babylonian exile till the birth of Jesus the Messiah (Matt 1:12–16). The basic thesis of this genealogy is that Jesus the Messiah comes to fulfill the mission and the dreams of both the Abrahamic covenant and the Davidic covenant.

What were the goals and the aspirations of these two covenants? This book will seek to address this crucial question.

While it is important to delineate the issues around the Abrahamic and Davidic covenants, the main focus of this genealogy is not on these. The main focus of the genealogy is on women. Five women are highlighted in the genealogy of Jesus the Messiah: Tamar (Matt 1:3), Rahab (Matt 1:5), Ruth (Matt 1:5), Uriah's wife (Matt 1:6), and Mary (Matt 1:16). Each of the five women are emblematic of different kinds of evil in society. This book will delineate different aspects of these evils in society, and then set out the justice solutions which the Bible proposes.

It delineates the #MeToo voices of five emblematic women.

Each of the five women also represents a different part of the Bible. Tamar represents the patriarchal era (Gen 38); Rahab represents the Exodus era (Josh 2); Ruth represents the period of the Judges (the book of Ruth); Uriah's wife represents the period of the kings and the prophets (2 Sam 11); and Mary represents the New Testament era (Matt 1:18–25).

Each of these eras represented different kinds of issues with which the biblical #MeToo movement needed to engage. Yet, there are also similarities and continuities underlined in the struggles of women in each of these eras.

ALL THE BEGETTINGS OF THE MEN OF THE #METOO MOVEMENT

The creation narrative in Genesis ends with the words, "These are the be-gettings of the heavens and the earth when they were created" (Gen 2:4). It is as if the heavens and earth are a couple, begetting the rest of the universe.

This word is used repeatedly in the book of Genesis, the "book of Be-gettings." It is used of men begetting. It is used of women begetting. It is used of creation begetting. It is as if all of creation is given the responsibility of begetting God's mission.

The book of Matthew, the first Gospel, also begins with begettings: "This is the book of the begettings of Jesus the Messiah, the son of David, the son of Abraham" (my translation). It is as if all the begettings of Genesis find their culmination in this final set of begettings in the Gospel of Mat-thew, and in the gospel of Jesus the Messiah.

Of course, it seems rather odd that creation and men also beget. In global society today, only women beget. In fact, in many parts of the world, that is the only function given to women—to beget, and to feed the babies and men. This is a very sad, global injustice against women.

In the Bible, by contrast, men are also given the responsibility of be-getting. This is a huge responsibility, and were this attitude to be adopted by men, I think it would cure many of the injustices that are done against women in our modern society, injustices which are highlighted by the #MeToo movement.

In Matthew 1, the issue of Matthew's #MeToo movement finds its place right in the middle of a string of begettings, phrases like, "Abraham begat, Isaac begat, Jacob begat," and so on. Each of the four women men-tioned in the Hebrew Bible are essentially a part of the #MeToo movement of the Bible. They are gentiles, the other. They are abused by men in power.

It seems clear to me that quite a crucial answer to the #MeToo crisis lies in a key principle seen in this "begettings genealogy." If only men would view sex as not merely an opportunity to experience pleasure at the expense of women, but rather as an opportunity to be a part of God's mission of begetting, there would be no sexual abuse of women.

ALL THE MARYS OF THE BIBLE

In linking Mary's name to that of the other four women of the Old Testament in the introduction, the New Testament makes it clear that the gospel of Jesus the Messiah squarely addresses the issues of evil and injustice raised in their stories. It also links with the story of Mary and the other women in the New Testament.

Mary's name is crucial because it is clearly a link to another crucial character in the Torah, whose name was also Mary. The texture of the book of Matthew leads us to see this clear link. The birth of Jesus in Matthew is followed by the same kind of massacre of baby boys which happened during the reign of the pharaoh of Exodus 2.

The ministry of Jesus, and particularly at the end of his life in the concluding section of Matthew, mentions several Marys who follow Jesus. Archaeological digs from the time of Jesus suggest that Mary was a very common name among the low classes of people groups called *am ha-aretz*. The obvious question that one may ask is, "Why is the name Mary so common during this time, and why is the name of Moses' sister Mary?"

Several sections of the Old Testament shed some light on this. The name Mary means "bitter." A good explanation for this may be seen in the narrative, when Naomi, . . . when Naomi, the mother-in-law of Ruth, goes back to Bethlehem from Moab, the women of Bethlehem exclaim, "That is Naomi!" Upon hearing this, she responds, "Don't call me *Naomi,* the Joyful One, call me *Mara,* the Bitter One!" (Ruth 1:19–21)

A study of history, both during the time of Moses and during the time of Jesus, makes it clear that the Egyptians during the time of Moses, and Romans during the time of Jesus, employed the raping of girls as a tool of war and subjugation. So, little girls were called Mary, or bitter. The parents mourned when a little baby girl was born, and they said, "I am so sorry you were born a girl. Your life will be bitter, Mary."

The Gospel of Matthew seeks to deal with issues which lead to these kinds of awful forms of injustice and evil, which all the Marys of history before the time of Jesus and during the time of Jesus endured. Women still face the same kinds of injustices and awful experiences even today.

The following chapters delineate the issues faced by Marys, then and now.

2

Tamar and the #MeToo Movement

The first instance of #MeToo highlighted in the genealogy of Jesus the Messiah is Tamar. She is a gentile Mary.[11] The narrative of Tamar is placed in a very interesting spot in the book of Genesis. Genesis 38 is squeezed between the Joseph narrative, Genesis 37 and 39. In Genesis 37, the seventeen-year-old Joseph tells his father about the "evil" that his brothers are doing (Gen 37:2). In Hebrew, the phrase *dibbah ra'* refers to systemic forms of evil, which was a part of the deep fabric of society during the patriarchal time. The next use of this word *dibbah* is found in Num 13:32; 14:36, 37. It refers to the nature of systemic evil that is found in Canaanite society and religion.

What is evil? The Tamar narrative, right in the middle of the Joseph narrative, addresses this question quite squarely. Genesis 37 ends with the words of the shocked and mourning Jacob, "It is my son's robe. An evil (*ra'*) animal has eaten him" (Gen 37:33, cf. 37:20). The narrative seems to make it clear that not only is human society evil, but this characteristic of evil finds its way into the animal kingdom, as well.[12]

The Genesis 38 narrative begins with Judah "going down (*yarad*)." In the Torah, "going down," is never a good thing. The name of the river Jordan (*yardan*) is derived from this verb *yarad*. It is a river that begins at the heights of Mount Hermon, goes through the Great Rift Valley, and finally

---

11. See Menn, *Judah and Tamar (Genesis 38)*.

12. In a later chapter, I will show that animals were used in human religions to do evil against women and girls.

ends in the Dead Sea. The Dead Sea is 1,412 feet below sea level. It is so highly saline that nothing can survive in this sea. Therefore, whenever the biblical author uses the word *yarad*, it is a literary device to say, "You are also going to end up in the Dead Sea, and you are going to die."

When he goes down he forcibly takes a Canaanite woman. The Hebrew does not say he marries her, as is translated in most English translations (Gen 38:2). He has three sons with him. His sons turn out to be people who do evil (*ra*) in the eyes of the LORD." (Gen 38:7, 10). It does not say what kind of evil. However, it becomes clear that this was evil of a sexual nature, in how they treated Canaanite women.

Judah sends Tamar away to live the life of a widow among the Canaanite people.[13] He knew that widows were the most vulnerable group of women in Canaanite society. He promises her that he will marry her to his son Selah, when he is ready. According to the ethics of the Torah, this was a legal practice called the law of levirate marriage. According to this law, the brother of the deceased husband must marry the widow, to protect her from all kinds of abuse suffered by widows in ancient societies (Deut 25:5–6).[14] According to this law, the firstborn son of this marriage was considered to be the son of the deceased brother, who would be responsible for the well-being of the widowed mother in her old age. Two of the sons of Judah died. The firstborn, who was the husband of Tamar, died because he did "evil in the eyes of the LORD." The narrative that follows makes it clear that this probably had to with how he abused and misused Tamar, which was a common practice in Canaanite society. The second son, Onan, had sexual encounters with Tamar, just to satisfy his sexual desires. The text in Hebrew makes it clear that he raped her, and did not want her to become

13. Research in world societies even today shows that widows are the among the most vulnerable group of people in the world. In the slum where I was reared, no one wanted to associate with a widow. A widow could never get remarried. She was considered to be a bad omen. A widow was generally sent back to the village from where she came and had to live apart from the rest of the village. Obviously, she was susceptible to human trafficking and evil men who would take advantage of her.

14. I have seen widows in India suffer much. No one wants to associate with them. Widows can never get married. There is an ancient practice in India where widows were either forced to commit suicide by jumping into the funeral pyre of their dead husbands, which was considered to be the honorable thing to do (this practice is called *sati*), or they had to live in a house far removed from civilization, with other widows. These widows were, of course, abused by sex traffickers. This awful situation is portrayed in a 2005 movie produced by Deepa Mehta, called *Water*. Ancient Near Eastern societies also practiced similar awful practices.

pregnant with a child who would carry on the name of his dead brother. He did not care about the welfare of Tamar. The text states that he also did "evil in the eyes of the LORD" (Gen 38:10), just like his older brother. What was the nature of this evil? Again, readings in Canaanite religion and society suggest that he abused and misused Tamar for his own sexual purposes, and for the sexual purposes of other men. The text simply says, for this reason, "the LORD put him to death" (Gen 38:7).

It seems like Judah was a participant in the evil of his sons, so he sent his daughter-in-law to her father's house to continue to endure her awful abuse. Then Tamar took matters into her own hands. She went to a popular place frequented by men of high stature. It was called Ennaim, the place between two wells. At this place, Judah had a sexual encounter with Tamar. He surmised that she was a "religious prostitute (*qadosha*)" (Gen 38:21, 22). Later, when he finds out that she is pregnant, he organizes her death sentence by public shaming and fire.

Thankfully, when he had sex with her, she had asked for "his signet, and cord, and staff" (Gen 38:18), three items of very personal identity. So when she produced them before the people he exclaimed, "she is more just (*Tsedakah*) than I" (Gen 38:26). Tamar bears twins, Perez and Zerah. Perez becomes the great forefather of Jesus the Messiah.

This narrative cannot be understood without a good understanding of ancient Near Eastern religions. Places like wells, *Ennaim*, and trees that surrounded the wells were sacred places where young girls and boys from low classes were forced to perform their sacred duties to goddesses like *Inanna*, *Ishtar*, and several other deities. Usually, the young girl or boy was forced to drink intoxicating drinks, called "holy" drinks, from various kinds of trees, usually grapes or fig trees, before they were forced to perform their religiously centered sexual duty.

Religious rituals with temple priestesses was very common in ancient Near Eastern religions. Even men known as *gala* wore women's clothing and performed sexual rituals on men as a part of the religious rituals. These would happen within the temple precincts, usually under sacred trees like grape vines or fig trees, and usually next to a well.

According to the Torah, any such practice of religious-oriented sexual prostitution was forbidden.

> None of the daughters of Israel shall be a cult prostitute (*qadesha*),
> and none of the sons of Israel shall be a cult prostitute (*qadesh*).
> You shall not bring the fee of a prostitute or the wages of a dog
> into the house of the LORD your God in payment for any vow, for
> both of these are an abomination to the LORD your God." (Deut
> 23:16–17)[15]

This practice of abusing girls and women was quite common in ancient Near Eastern religions. It was also common in other parts of the world.

Aryan Hinduism also venerates the *Nyagrodha*, or fig tree. From the fruit of this tree, boys and girls were given the intoxicating drink of divinity called *Soma*. When they were drunk, Hindu priests would then participate in ritual sex with them. This ritual sex happened under these ancient fig trees called *Nyagrodha* (Rigveda 8.48.3). When the high-caste men drink the *soma* and meditate under these trees, they experience divinity. According to the *Matsaya sutra*, when gurus have religiously oriented sex with *Shudra* (low-caste, slave) women under these trees, they experience healing, and are able to have children. Other girls are forced to devote their lives to the worship of the peepal tree, and the god Vishnu who resides in the peepal tree. These girls are called *Devadasis*, a Hindu form of sacred prostitution. Sex as a part of religious rituals, it is thought, will result in *moksha*, or salvation.[16]

In the biblical narrative, it may be noted that when Judah has a sexual encounter with Tamar, he promises her a "young goat" (Gen 38:20). The Hebrew words for this animal, *gedi 'azim*, are used to describe an animal sacrifice (Judg 6:9; 13:15). This makes it clear that the goal of Judah's sexual encounter was more than that. He was seeking to worship the fertility gods of Canaanite society.

It may also be noted that Tamar asks for his "signet, cord, and staff" (Gen 38:18). These were all the marks of his identity and authority. The signet (*chotam*) is a mark of kingly authority (Jer 22:24; Hag 2:23), the cord (*patil*) is a mark of priestly authority (Exod 28:37; 39:21), and the staff (*Mateh*) is a mark of prophetic authority (Exod 4:17, 20; Num 20:9, 11).

15. Sadly, even animals like goats and dogs were used in these acts of sexuality in religious practices of Egypt and other ancient Near Eastern religions. See Ray, "Animal Cults," 90.

16. Shingal, "Devadasi System," 107–23.

Judah, it seems, is willing to forgo his complete identity for the sake of this sexual ritual.

Following this, Judah seeks to keep his part of the deal. He sends his people to give Tamar the young goat sacrifice, but they cannot find the "temple priestess, (*qadesha)*" (Gen 38:21).

Three months after this, word comes to Judah that Tamar has prostituted herself, and she is now pregnant because of her prostitution (Gen 38:24). Judah's response is rather telling. He pronounces the death sentence on her: "death by burning" (Genesis 38:24). It should be noted that nowhere does the Torah prescribe "death by burning." Deuteronomy 22:23 does call for community punishment—after a trial—at the city gate for both the man and the woman who have committed the act of adultery. Death by burning, however, was a common Canaanite practice.

The second issue involves Judah coming to a decision without even asking for the identity of the man who was involved in the sexual intercourse. This is very similar to the situation in John 8 where the Pharisees brought a woman to Jesus who was "caught in the act of adultery" (John 8:3). The obvious question is, "Where is the man?"

The narrative, tellingly, answers this question. She says, "Identify these things—the signet, the cord and the staff. By, this person, I am pregnant" (Gen 38:26).

Judah immediately recognizes those crucial symbols of his authority, and he declares, "She is more just than I." The Hebrew word *Tsdakah* is a crucial word of justice which was supposed to be the purview of the king, priest and prophet. In this simple, yet powerful sentence, Tamar is elevated to the highest authority.

The narrative makes it clear that Tamar, the Mary of this Genesis narrative does this courageously, justly, and in an unorthodox manner. She fulfills all the laws of the Torah by her courageous action, even though she is a gentile. The descendants of Abraham, Isaac, and Jacob failed in bringing about justice, but Tamar took matters in her own hands and fulfilled all the laws of the Torah. She was declared to be *Tsadiq*, or Just person. The only other person of whom this was said is Abraham in Genesis 15:6: "Abraham believed the LORD, and he was declared to be just (a *Tsadiq*)."

Tamar has everything stacked against her, and yet now the narrative declares that she, a low-class Canaanite, has achieved the highest goal of the Torah. Tamar is elevated to the status of being the mother of the Messiah's predecessor, when the narrative makes it plain that Judah, "did not know her again" (Gen 38:26 and Matt 1:25), just like Joseph did not know Mary, till the birth of Jesus.

The Tamar narrative is indeed a very powerful one. It shows how women, usually from low classes of society, were sexually abused, many times in situations which were religiously sanctioned by the higher classes of society, usually the kingly-priestly class. This was true in the ancient Near East, and it remains true in many societies today.

Yet women like Tamar, in spite of all the odds set against them, have overcome!

The Bible declares Tamar to be "the Just #MeToo Woman."

This powerful narrative is a part of the Bible's original #MeToo movement.

3

Rahab and the #MeToo Movement

The second #MeToo highlighted in the genealogy of Jesus is Rahab, another gentile Mary.

The narrative of Rahab is found in the context of a people who are about to enter into the promised land. It is a new generation. The previous generation died in the wilderness because they "did not believe" in the promise of God (Num 13 and 14, esp. 14:11). Moses, the great leader and the great law giver, was also dead because "he did not believe" in God to declare him as the Just One (*Qadosh*) in the eyes of the people (Num 20:12).

A life of faith, (*Amen*) was considered to be a central virtue of the community, which had recently been saved from slavery, including sexual slavery of their women.

The Lord tells Moses that another person will lead the next generation into the promised land. He tells them that when they go into the promised land, their mission is to missionally "possess (*Yarash*)" all the people (Num 33:51, 52, 53, 55). Unfortunately, most English translations—namely the KJV, NIV, ESV, and NRSV—translate this word with violent words like "drive out." Throughout the Hebrew Bible, *yarash* means "to possess" in a very positive sense. Psalm 37:11, for example, says, "The meek will possess, (*yarash*) the land," and Psalm 37:29 says, "The just will possess the land." The noun form of this verb is used of someone who peacefully inherits the property (Gen 15:3, 8; 27:28; 28:4). When God appears to Moses in the wilderness, he says to him, "I will bring you into the land I swore to give to Abraham, to Isaac, and to Jacob. I will give it to you for a possession

(*Yarash*). I am the LORD" (Exod 6:8). This is the sense of the verb and the noun throughout the Torah.

Now that Moses is dead, Joshua—the next leader—sends two scouts into the promised land. It should not surprise the reader that the first person they encounter is the most dispossessed person: Rahab, a prostitute. Why was Rahab's house at the corner of the city? Obviously, because she belonged to the periphery of Canaanite society. In ancient Near Eastern religions, the demoness Rahab is associated with the demoness Tiamat. She is partly a woman, and partly a fish. Other parts of the Old Testament also describe Rahab as an ogress or demoness.

In ancient Near Eastern religions, lower-level girls and women were used as temple prostitutes to serve the priests of different societies. In Canaanite religion, that was true of Rahab. Women like Rahab were used to serve goddesses like Rahab and *Tannin,* the goddess of the sea. These women are religious sexual slaves. Divine kings and priests would worship the images of goddesses like Rahab and Tannin. They would get possessed by the spirits of these goddesses, and in this state of trance they would have religious sex with women, usually called Rahab. These injustices are religiously sanctioned, making this a systemic evil of a very deep kind.

In the Rahab narrative of Joshua 2, the two scouts are sent into the land with the following command, "Go, see the land, especially Jericho" (Josh 2:1). The two verbs here combine two crucial junctures in the history of humanity. The first imperative, "go," reminded the people of the Abraham commission "to go," and to be a blessing (Gen 12:1). In the second imperative, they were asked to "see" just like God "saw" seven times in the creation narrative (Gen 1:4, 10, 12, 18, 21, 25, 31). Each time "God sees it was good." The final time, when God created humanity, God sees that it is "very good." It is as if the creation narrative is saying that humanity which has gender, racial, etc. equality is a very good human human society.

In Genesis 1, seeing is an act of discerning and judging. In contrast to Genesis 1, where everything is peaceful, just, and good, the two scouts "see" religiously oriented evil and prostitution of low-class people like Rahab. Rahab is not a prostitute because she chooses to be a prostitute. She is a prostitute because she is enslaved to the goddess Rahab. She lived at the wall of the city of Jericho. When she hid the scouts that Joshua had sent, she proclaimed that the power of the LORD was greater than the power of the divine kings and religions of the Egyptians, and of all the people groups around them:

I know that the LORD has given you the land, and that the fear of
you has fallen upon us, and that all the inhabitants of the land melt
away before you. For we have heard how the LORD dried up the
water of the Red Sea before you when you came out of Egypt, and
what you did to the two kings of the Amorites who were beyond
the Jordan, to Sihon and Og, whom you regarded as *Cherem* (devoted people or things). (Josh 2:8–9)

There was an acknowledgment that two supernatural powers were
pitted against each other. One was the supernatural power of YHWH, and
on the other side were the supernatural powers of the gods and goddesses
of the Egyptians, Canaanites, and other people groups. Therefore, Rahab
asked for a "sign." (Josh 2:12) This is no ordinary sign. The Hebrew phrase,
Ot Emet refers to a true and sure sign of the power of God. The cosmos was
a sign of the power of God (Gen 1:14). All the miracles which God did in
Egypt were signs of the supernatural power of God over the supernatural
signs of the gods of Egypt (Exod 4:8, 9; 7:3; 12:13; Deut 6:22; 11:3; 34:11,
etc.). Rahab knew that she needed a supernatural sign to be delivered from
religious and systemic slavery. The supernatural sign that was given her
(Josh 2:18) was the same as the sign which was given to the Exodus community when they were delivered from the hand of the divine king, pharaoh
(Exod 12:13). The capture of Jericho is depicted as a divine sign. How else
could the mere blowing of a *shofar* cause the walls of Jericho to fall? When
the Israelites entered into Jericho in Joshua 6, they were supposed to be saving those people who belonged to the enslaved people groups—the Rahabs
of Canaanite society. They were supposed to be destroying everything that
represented the evil and unjust religions of Jericho. These are called "the
devoted things (*Cherem*)" (Josh 6:17, 18). Unfortunately, in the history that
followed this dramatic event, the children of Israel also devoted themselves
to these *Cherem*, the very same religious practices which resulted in so
much injustice and sexual trafficking (Josh 7:1, 11, 12). Sadly, these unjust
religious practices became a pattern in Israelite society for a long time (1
Sam 15:21).

Rahab was not merely saved from prostitution. She was saved from
religiously oriented sexual slavery. Sadly, the children of Israel adopted all
the evil practices of the people and cultures of the ancient Near East.

Rahab's courageous action was a #MeToo action.

The New Testament claims her to be a Mother of faith (Heb 11:31).
Day after day, night after night, she stayed on the periphery of the city, the

city wall, where the royalty and soldiers would come and abuse her, all in the name of religiously sanctioned propriety. She knew that this was the lot of her whole family, especially the girls in her family. She knew that the only way for her to gain freedom from her awful situation of being abused by Canaanite men was to trust in a God who cares for and saves slaves, including sexual slaves. Therefore, she gave refuge to two representatives of the enslaved community. She took the courageous step to lie to the fearsome Canaanite militia. She knew that she was asking for death should they be found.

Rahab's final #MeToo sign was to hang the "scarlet chord" from her window. In Hebrew the color scarlet is synonymous with "red like blood." (Isa 1:18). It is a color which is emblematic of much violence and bloodshed. Yet, this is the color that the Exodus community put on the door posts of their dwelling places—the blood of the Pesach lamb (Exod 12:7, 13, 22). It was a sign of their faith in God, who would deliver them from slavery. It was also the color of the intoxicating drink that women were given before the religious sexual rituals were performed. This is the #MeToo sign which Rahab put on her window, to gain salvation from so much pain and sexual slavery. What an act of bravery! What a transformation of the sign!

Rahab the prostitute was elevated to be the Mother of the Israelites. According to Jewish tradition, Rahab was the great-great-grandmother of the prophet Jeremiah (Num Rabbah 8:9). He was a prophet who constantly fought against wrongs being done to women. According to the rabbis, she also became a great model for prayer. So the rabbis opine that when Hezekiah was sick to the point of death and prayed with his face to the wall (*qir*), it was the city wall on which Rahab lived (Jerusalem Talmud 4:4, 8).

Rahab, the gentile woman, also called a prostitute, is another amazing model of the original #MeToo movement in the Bible.

4

Ruth and the #MeToo Movement

BACKGROUND TO THE RUTH NARRATIVE

The book of Ruth finds its place in two different places in the Old Testament. The English Old Testament follows the ordering of books as found in the Greek translation called the LXX. In this, the book of Ruth follows the book of Judges. In the Hebrew Bible, the book of Ruth follows the Books of Proverbs, Job, and Song of Songs, and it is followed by Lamentations, Ecclesiastes, and Esther. Each of these placements of the book of Ruth gives a different picture of Ruth, and the #MeToo movement, as seen in the story of Ruth. In the LXX ordering of the book of Ruth, it follows the storyline we have seen in the analysis of the narrative of Rahab.

The book of Judges, which follows the book of Joshua, constantly concludes with the following phrase, "In those days there was no king in Israel. Each man of renown did what was right in their own eyes" (Judg 21:25). This is a constant refrain in the book of Judges: 17:6; 18:1; 19:1. The ethics of the people were not led by the Torah of the God who took them out of slavery and gave them the ethic. Rather, each "person of renown" (*Ish*) decided what was ethical based on his own judgment. Another constant refrain in the book of Judges is:

26

And the people of Israel did what was evil (*ra'*) in the eyes of the
Lord. They served the Baals, the Ashtoreth, the gods of Syria, the
gods of Moab, the gods of the Ammonites, the gods of the Philis-
tines. They forsook the LORD, and did not serve him. (Judg 10:6;
2:11; 3:7, 12; 4:1; 6:1; 13:1).

Obviously, the ethic of the *Ish*, the high-class people, was derived from
the ethics of these people groups. The ethics of these people groups were
based on the worship of gods and goddesses who demanded the sexual
slavery of boys and girls.

The god Baal is described as a bull who during his time in the neth-
erworld made love to a heifer, mounting her about eighty times (KTU 1.5
v:18–21)[17]. The word Baal itself means "husband." Therefore, women were
"married" to this god and men had sex with them in the process of the
worship of Baal. In reality, women had religiously oriented sex with priests
of Baal. These women were told that this was the only way in which they
could have children from their own husbands, when the time came. Their
primary husband (*Baal*) was the god *Baal*. This was the main god of the
Moabites (Num 23:28; Josh 13:20).

The ethics of the people of Israel is seen in its most horrible form at the
end of the book of Judges, in connection with the worship of Baal at *Baal
Tamar* (Judg 20:33). Here *Baal* was worshipped under date palms (*Tamar*).
Judges 19–20 describes a dreadful set of events. A Levite was traveling with
his concubine. (This is rather odd because in ancient Near Eastern societies
a concubine was a sexual slave. Usually, aristocratic people and divine kings
owned concubines). The fact that a Levite, who was supposed to be serving
in the tabernacle of YHWH, would own a sexual slave, speaks volumes
about the very low ethics of Israelite society. The Levite is from Ephraim in
the middle of Israel. The concubine is from Bethlehem, in the south. This
is crucial to note, because later, David will emerge from Bethlehem, a city
with a market for sexual slaves. In Judges 19:2, the sexual slave, who is not
named, leaves the Levite to go and live in her father's house in Bethlehem.
The reason behind this is debated in translations. The NIV and ESV read
that his concubine "was unfaithful to him," but the KJV translates it as,
"played the whore against him." It seems to me that the NIV and the ESV
simply follow the KJV in this translation, and it just continues the attitude

---

17. *Keilalphabetische Texte aus Ugarit*, or KTU, is a very common abbreviation in
Ancient Near Eastern Studies. See, for example, van der Toorn et al., *Dictionary of Deities
and Demons*, 37.

that male societies have towards certain groups of women. It seems to me that the NRSV gets is right. It reads, "his concubine became angry with him." The LXX simply says, "she departed from him." The NRSV and the LXX translation are based on cognate languages like Akkadian, where the verb *zenu*, means "to be angry, or to protest." It seems to me the NRSV and the LXX give a better sense of the essential meaning of the Hebrew verb and the noun, *zanah*. It suggests that the act of *zanah* is an angry protest against the Levite, who abused her. This is quite a #MeToo action.

This is quite a daring step that the woman makes, especially in the context of society at that time. I have known several situations, even today in India, Pakistan, and the Middle East, where when a woman is abused she has no recourse. She cannot return back to her father's house because she will only experience more abuse there. She is constantly told, by everyone concerned, that she has no option. She has to continue to suffer the abuse.

Sadly, abuse in these societies begins at a very young age, usually when the girl begins her first menstrual cycles. When the girl becomes a sexual slave, she is considered to be a prostitute. Global research in prostitution suggests that 85 to 95 percent of those in prostitution were sexually assaulted as children.[18] There is much material on this. Melissa Farley, clinical psychologist, and director of prostitution research and education at the Kaiser Foundation Research Institute in Oakland, California, has compiled the work of clinical psychologists in nine countries in *Prostitution, Trafficking, and the Traumatic Stress*. This volume makes it clear that globally, prostitution is violence, and it results in lifelong trauma for the girls and boys ensnared in this horror. They are trapped for life in this cycle. Prostitution leaves women and children physically, mentally, emotionally, and spiritually devastated for life.

The next phase of this Judges narrative is even more bizarre. The Levite takes his sexual slave from her father's house. On the way between Bethlehem and Ephraim, they had to go by Jerusalem. However, Jerusalem is regarded by the Levite to be a "city of foreigners (*Nokri*)" (Judg 19:12) so he does not go into Jerusalem. This decision of the Levite is interesting because in the Bible it is the strangers, the *nokri*, who are most vulnerable to abuse and human trafficking.

Both in ancient societies and today, *Nokri* are foreign women who are sexually abused and prostituted. In the Bible, sadly, this is what King Solomon did. He gathered hundreds of "foreign women (*nashim nokriyot*)"

18. Hunter, "Prostitution is Cruelty and Abuse," 99.

(1 Kgs 11:1). These women were Moabites, Ammonites, Edomites, Hittites, etc. (1 Kgs 11). These were sexual slaves who were also religious sexual slaves through whom Solomon worshipped sexually oriented gods and goddesses (1 Kgs 11:8). Sadly, this abuse of foreign women was also practiced by the Jewish men in exile (Ezra 10). The prophets Ezra and Nehemiah castigated them for this awful practice.

For whatever reason, the Levite did not want to go into the city of *Nokri*. Rather, he went to Gebeah, a city of the Benjamites. Had he gone to the city of foreigners, she would have been safe, but it seems like he was not thinking of her, but rather of his own well-being.

As it turns out, no one in Gebeah offered them a place to stay, so they were homeless. Interestingly, an old man who himself was a stranger (*Ger*), a migrant worker, gave them refuge for the night. He said to them, "Please do not spend the night in the broad space (*Rechov*)" (Judg 19:20). It may be observed that this Hebrew word is related to *Rahab*, a name for the goddess of prostitution.[19] This could well have been the space for open prostitution and the old foreigner wanted to save them from the danger that lay in that place. It is crucial to note that the #MeToo movement of the Bible had numerous allies, many of whom were men who had also experienced much abuse, like this old man.

In the next sequence, while the strangers are having dinner, the "worthless men (*beliyya'al*)" (Judg 19:20) of Benjamin bang on the door, demanding to have sex with the Levite. It must be noted that the words *beliya'al* and *Baal* go together, intentionally so. The allegiance to *Baal* leads to multiple forms of abuse. This Hebrew word is always used of men who are intent on sexually abusing people of whom they can take advantage (e.g. the sons of Eli, who raped women—women who came to worship God [1 Sam 1:16]). It should be noted that this is what the men of Sodom and Gomorrah wanted to do with the men who visited Abraham and Lot (Gen 19).

The old man pleads with them not to do this "evil thing (*ra'*)" (Judg 19:23). In another weird sequence, he offers them his virgin daughter and the Levite's concubine. This, sadly, was a common happening in ancient Near Eastern religions and cultures. Girls of foreigners were always abused. Did the strangers and foreigners give into the extreme pressure of the religions and cultures around them? One would never know.

---

19. For example, in commenting on Job 9:13 and 26:12, D. J. A. Clines suggests that Rahab should be considered the Ancient Near Eastern mythic sea goddess ("Job," 467). See also Day, *God's Conflict with the Dragon*; Spronk, "Rahab," 684–86.

In the slum in New Delhi where I was reared, this was a common happening. High-caste men would come to the huts of the low-caste people when they heard the girl had become a woman, i.e., she had just begun her menstrual cycle. My low-caste and outcast friends knew that this was coming. They were owned by the high-caste person. It was a debt that they would not have been able to pay for several generations. This was the only way, they were made to believe, they could pay off some of the debt. So they would just give into the money lender who was standing outside their hut.

After the virgin girl was taken, they would beat their chests and weep bitterly, but, they had no social, political, or religious power to refuse the high-caste lender. The virgin daughter had no power to say anything, and likewise in this narrative, the virgin daughter and the concubine had no power to say anything.

But it seems like the concubine stepped forward, which saved the life of the old man's virgin daughter. The young men of Benjamin gang raped the woman all night long. In the morning, she was found dead at the doorstep of the house where the Levite was lodging. What an act of courage by this young woman! She sacrificed her life to save the life of another young girl.

The Levite's response to this is quite bizarre. He cuts her body into twelve parts and scatters it across the twelve tribes of Israel. This bizarre act causes a bloody war between the rest of the tribes of Israel and the sons of Benjamin. After much back and forth and bloodshed on both sides, finally the rest of the tribes were victorious over the sons of Benjamin. The narrative, though, takes on another bizarre turn. The tribes of Israel regard the action of the sons of Benjamin to be evil (*ra'*) (Judg 20:12, 13).

Is war a solution? It seems like violence only leads to more violence, and bloodshed. It does not address the central issues involved, in the question asked by the abused, and now dead, young woman.

Their solution was a pact in which they decided not to give their daughters in marriage to the sons of Benjamin. Ironically, this causes them consternation, because they now realize that the tribe of Benjamin will have no progeny. So, they come up with an awful alternative plan. They tell the sons of Benjamin about a ritual practice in Baal worship. In this ritual, the daughters of Shiloh, drunk from much wine, dance a sexual ritual dance in the vineyards. Therefore, they are told:

> Go and lie in ambush in the vineyards and watch. If the daughters
> of Shiloh come out to dance in the dances, then come out of the

vineyards and snatch each man his woman from the daughters
of Shiloh, and go to the land of Benjamin . . . And the people of
Benjamin did so and lifted up their women, according to their
number, from the dancers whom they carried off. (Judg 21:21, 23)

The dance here is no ordinary dance. The Hebrew word, *chul*, is a
twisting, writhing, shaking, almost in travail, kind of dance, and so in this
the dancing girls experience a kind of euphoria and hallucinate. When they
are in this state, high-class men and kings have religiously oriented sexual
encounters with them.

In English translations, what is happening here is usually translated
as, "So that is what the Benjamites did. While the young women were dancing, each man caught one and carried her off to be his wife. Then they
returned to their inheritance and rebuilt the towns and settled in them
(Judg 21:23 NIV)." This itself is quite bizarre, but the Hebrew text is quite
stark. They did not marry these women. They "lifted them up (*nasa'*) into a
state of ritual prostitution." The Aramaic translation of Judges 21:23 reads,
"They transgressed the decree of the Memra of the LORD and lifted up for
themselves foreign women from the house of Moab."

This word, *nasa'*, when used in the context of another person, always
has negative connotations. This what the exiled people did to the women
among whom they were living (Ezra 10:44), just because that is what
they did in the Babylonian and Persian religions. In 2 Chronicles 11:21,
Rehoboam "lifted up" eighteen women and sixty sexual slaves. Similarly,
Abijah "lifted up" fourteen women (2 Chr 13:21). Most English translations
translated these as marriage to women. However, it becomes clear that
these were all considered to be illegitimate religious liaisons with women.

In the worship of Baal, Asherah, Ishtar, Inanna, and other gods and
goddesses of ancient Near Eastern society, certain groups of women performed the task of satisfying these gods and goddesses through sexual rituals. In doing so, they ritually carried the offenses of these ancient societies
upon themselves, and so appeased them. Therefore, Baal, Ishtar, etc., provided fertility for the people and the land.

In the context of the Old Testament and the ancient Near Eastern religions, it becomes clear that the sons of Benjamin did not merely marry
Moabite women. They used them as temple prostitutes.

Why is this background important? Because, we shall see that the sons
of Elimelech in the book of Ruth did the same thing to Moabite women.

Thankfully, Ruth remains to tell her #MeToo story.

31

THE RUTH NARRATIVE IN THE CONTEXT OF THE PROPHETS

In the LXX and English translations of the Bible, the book of Ruth follows the book of Judges. Judges ends with a group of women, the daughters of Shiloh, being used as temple prostitutes. Poignantly, Ruth 1:4 revisits this same scenario, as if to say that this was not merely a trait of the sons of Benjamin, but rather a common practice in Israel.

Most English translations read that the sons of Elimelech and Naomi, "married Moabite women, one named Orpah and the other Ruth" (Ruth 1:4 NIV). Right off the bat, the Hebrew word in the Ruth narrative is *nasa'*, i.e. they did not marry them, but rather "lifted them up" into temple prostitution. They did this in Moab for ten years.

The Hebrew phrase for marriage is, "(The man's name) takes (the woman's name) and she became his wife." This is what Boaz does in Ruth 4:13. This pattern is seen throughout the Bible with reference to the marriage of Abraham and Sarah (Gen 20:12), the marriage of Isaac and Rebekah (Gen 24:67), David and Abigail (1 Sam 25:42), and so on. This narrative makes it quite clear that the two sons of Elimelech and Naomi just did to Ruth and Naomi what the people of Moab already did to women in the context of the fertility-related gods and goddesses.

The Ruth narrative makes it clear, right at the outset, that societies can quite easily and quickly fall into systems of evil. It becomes especially easy in the context of hardship. In this case, there is famine in Bethlehem. Ironically, Bethlehem literally means, "house of bread." The Hebrew text seems to stress this irony. Ruth 1:1 suggests that the prominent family of Bethlehem seeks to go on a "sojourn" in the land of Moab. However, they "become there," i.e. they become a part of the culture and religion of the Moabites (Ruth 1:2). This is what leads to the evil actions of the sons of Elimelech. Evil reaches a horrible level, when society normalizes it, and it is no longer regarded as evil. However, after the sons die, Naomi decides to return to Bethlehem, because she hears that the LORD had visited his people, and had given them *lechem,* bread.

On the way, there is a crucial dialogue which takes place between Naomi and her daughters-in-law, Ruth and Orpah. She urges them to return to their "mother's house" (Ruth 1:8). Obviously, it has pained Naomi to see how her sons have abused Ruth and Orpah. So, she urges them to go back to the place of comfort—their "mother's house." (cf. Song 3:4; 8:2). Naomi describes what they have gone through as being bitter (*mara*).

Orpah returns to Moabite life, but Ruth sticks with Naomi. Naomi, though, continues to urge Ruth to return. She says, "See your sister-in-law has gone back to her people and her gods, return after your sister-in-law" (Ruth 1:15). Ruth's response is quite poignant:

> Do not urge me to leave you or to return from following you. For where you go I will go, and where you lodge I will lodge. Your people shall be my people, and your God my God. Where you die I will die, and there will I be buried. May the LORD do so to me and more also if anything but death parts me from you. (Ruth 1:16–17 ESV)

It seems clear the Ruth is making a definite choice not to return to her own people because she would still be treated as a temple prostitute. The dilemma she faces is would she be considered as a foreigner temple prostitute (*nakar*) in the new land, where she would be a refugee? Once your own people have taken advantage of you, other people in other lands are bound to doubly take advantage of you. This is especially true since the person to whom she is related is considered to be a social liability.

In Ruth 2, we find a counterculture situation. There is a person named Boaz who lets poor people come into his fields and pick from the produce. This is a counterculture situation. Bethlehem is a place which has just come out of famine, yet there is a person who does not care about hoarding wealth. Instead, he lets poor people into his fields to pick from his produce.

NARRATIVE OF RUTH AND THE #METOO PRINCIPLE IN THE TORAH

In Jewish liturgy the narrative of Ruth and Deuteronomy 26 are sung on *Shavuot*, the Feast of Weeks. It is also called latter firstfruits.

In the casuistic laws that they are given, which are based on this apodictic core found in the Ten Commandments, they are clearly told that there should not be any distinction between natives and foreigners: "You must have the same regulations for both the foreigner and the native-born" (Num 9:14 NIV). Then again, "Do not deprive the foreigner or the fatherless of justice, or take the cloak of the widow as a pledge" (Deut 24:17 NIV). And again, "Cursed is anyone who withholds justice from the foreigner, the fatherless or the widow" (Deut 27:19 NIV). There are numerous laws which stressed they had to always practice justice and equality with anyone who was "other," whether they be a people of different race, gender, or whatever.

This code of ethic was also stressed in their liturgy. On the first day of the Passover week (Sunday), the freed people celebrated the firstfruits. This happened in the first month of the biblical calendar. On this day, the people bring the firstfruit offerings into the presence of the LORD, and they recite the following passage from the book of Deuteronomy:

> My father was a wandering Aramean, and he went down into Egypt with a few people and lived there and became a great nation, powerful and numerous. But the Egyptians mistreated us and made us suffer, subjecting us to harsh labor. Then we cried out to the LORD, the God of our ancestors, and the LORD heard our voice and saw our misery, toil and oppression. So the LORD brought us out of Egypt with a mighty hand and an outstretched arm, with great terror and with signs and wonders. He brought us to this place and gave us this land, a land flowing with milk and honey; and now I bring the firstfruits of the soil that you, LORD, have given me." Place the basket before the LORD your God and bow down before him. Then you and the Levites and the foreigners residing among you shall rejoice in all the good things the LORD your God has given to you and your household. (Deut 26:1, 2, 5–11 NIV)

During this crucial time, which falls during the Passover Week (in the Christian calendar, this is the Holy Week), the people are told to always remember that their forefathers were "wandering Arameans." They were Gypsies who were unjustly treated and enslaved by the Egyptians. Yet God heard the cries of the enslaved people and saved them. This liturgy was to be celebrated by everybody of every race and gender. They brought this firstfruits offering to remind them that they must never have any kind of discrimination amongst themselves, against the weak and the marginalized, "the widow, the orphan, and the alien" (Deut 26:11).

This is the context of Ruth 2. It seems like Boaz was the only person who really practiced the liturgical text, Deuteronomy 26, and the context of the Ten Commandments. These remembrances would contrast with the systemic evil and discrimination which had seeped into Bethlehemite society from the societies of the surrounding people groups.

The laws in the Torah that dealt with firstfruits offerings made it clear that the poor and the foreigners were supposed to have equal access to the produce. "When you reap the harvest of your land, do not reap to the very edges of your field or gather the gatherings of your harvest. Leave them for the poor and for the foreigner residing among you. I am the LORD your

God" (Lev 23:22). This legal and economic system is found in several other places in the Torah e.g., Lev 19:9, 10. The Hebrew word *laqat*, "to gather," refers to gathering from the best, not merely from the refuse. It is the same word, which is used for the people "gathering" sumptuously of the LORD's provision in the wilderness (Exod 16; Num 11). Or, the "gathering" from God's gracious and good giving (Ps 104:28).

The laws in the Torah regarding the land, were indeed supposed to bring justice to the widows, the orphans, and the foreigners. In Leviticus 19:9–10, it says, "When you gather the harvest, you shall not gather your land right up to its extremity." And again, "You shall leave them for the poor, and for the sojourner. I am the LORD" (Lev 23:22).

This was the Torah's way of making sure that there would not be any poverty or hunger in society, no matter what the reason, whether it be famine or sickness or disability. It becomes clear that the laws of the Torah, especially with regard to women and foreigners, was designed to stand alongside and on behalf of the #MeToo victims of that time.

The laws regarding the land were also about the relationship between human beings and the land. They were supposed to bring justice to the land. This was based on the principle that the land was God's creation. When God created the land (*Ha Aretz*), he consistently called everything "good" and "very good" (Gen 1:4, 10, 12, 18, 21, 25, 31). Then God commissioned humanity with what is generally called the Missio Humanity, "Be fruitful, and multiply, and fill the land (*Ha Aretz*)" (Gen 1:28a). Unfortunately, the English translations then give authority to human beings to "have dominion over the fish of the sea, and over the birds of the heavens, and over the livestock, and over all the land (*Ha Aretz*), and over every creeping thing that creeps on the land (*Ha Aretz*)" (Gen 1:28b).

It should be noted that the Hebrew word *Ha Aretz* can be translated as "the earth" as well as "the land." I prefer "the land." Creation of the land is emblematic of the creation of the whole earth. Consequently, what human beings do to the land impacts the whole earth.

The creation text in Genesis blesses humanity and gives human beings the responsibility to take care of the land, because this will in turn help them take care of each other. In Genesis 1:28, God blesses humanity and says, "Be fruitful and increase in number; fill the earth and subdue it. Rule over the fish in the sea and the birds in the sky and over every living creature that moves on the ground" (Gen 1:28 NIV).

It should also be noted that the English phrase "to subdue and to rule over" is generally considered to be rather violent wording. It is what dictators do. They dominate and pillage. Unfortunately, it is women who are at the worst end of this subduing and ruling over. In history, sadly, Christian and Jewish kings have used this text as a pretext to do horrible things to women. In connection with this it should be noted that the Hebrew word *radah* is not a violent, domineering word. *Radah* is used to describe the gentle messianic rule of the Messiah, as found in Psalm 72:8, "May he have dominion, *radah*, from sea to sea, and from the river, to the ends of the earth." Indeed, when God gives laws regarding the care for the widows, orphans, and strangers, he constantly reminds the people not to rule (*radah*) ruthlessly, but rather rule gently and justly (Lev 25:43, 46, 53), just like the gentle and just Messiah himself.

The Torah gives specific rules to treat the land with honor and dignity, because the land is called "holy" (Exod 15:17). The people are given the Sabbath principle to honor the holiness of the land. This would lead to treating each other with honor and dignity.

The people are told that if they do not treat the land as holy; if they do not take care of the widows, poor, orphans, and strangers in the holy land;if they follow the evil practices of other religions, like sacrificing children to Molech and giving their daughters and sons as temple prostitutes, then the land will be desecrated, and she will vomit them. The Torah makes it clear that previous nations and people groups were "vomited" out by the "land," when they desecrated it (Lev 18:24–30).

In order to dignify the land, the people were also given the *Shmita* or "release" principle for the seventh year, (*Shevi'it*) (Deut 15:1–6). It was a "Sabbath of Sabbaths for the land" (Lev 25:4). Just like human beings—all human beings, including the poor and foreigners, and animals—the land was also supposed to be given a Sabbath rest. This was so the poor, the needy, and the orphans could eat from it (Exod 23:10–11).

The people are further told to proclaim a general amnesty in the fiftieth year—seven weeks of years, seven times seven years (Lev 25:8). This is also called the Year of Jubilee, when the *Shofar*, the ram's horn, will be blown, and everything, including the land, will return back to its original state, as in Genesis 1.

These laws regarding the land were given so that children, orphans, and women would not be put in a place where men would take advantage of them. The narrative of Ruth shows that Boaz observed the deep principles of these laws. Unfortunately, the rest of Israel could not care less about these laws. Throughout the history of Israel, the land was desecrated. As a result of this, evil things were done to the poor and the marginalized. Prophets like Jeremiah kept warning the people (e.g., Jer 7, 17, 29), and yet the kings and the leaders did not heed the words of the prophets. Therefore, the people were driven into exile.

The very last book of the Hebrew Bible, the book of Chronicles, describes the exile of the people in these words:

> He carried into exile to Babylon the remnant, who escaped from the sword, and they became servants to him and his successors until the kingdom of Persia came to power. The land enjoyed its Sabbath rests; all the time of its desolation it rested, until the seventy years were completed in fulfillment of the word of the LORD spoken by Jeremiah. (2 Chr 36:20, 21 NIV)

This is a very sad ending to the history of a people who were taken out of slavery and were given laws which would dignify the poor, the orphan, the widow, the stranger, and yes, even the land. Sadly, the people of Israel committed the same evils the Sumerians, the Canaanites, and other nations did. So the land vomited them out, and then enjoyed its Sabbath rest.

The narrative of Ruth makes it clear that there is an intrinsic connection between God, human beings, and the land (creation). When human beings do evil to each other, it desecrates the land (creation). When human beings do evil to the land (creation), it impacts other human beings. When human beings do evil to creation and to each other, it impacts their relationship with God.

These three are primary entities: God, land, and humanity. When human beings do evil to any one of these entities, it impacts the other, in a rather mystical way. The laws of the Torah were given to maintain a healthy and invigorating relationship between these three primary entities. The narrative of Ruth shows Boaz as a great example of one who lived by principles which maintained a good and healthy relationship between the three primary entities. He did this by coming alongside Ruth, the Moabite #MeToo woman.

RUTH ENCOUNTERS BOAZ AND THE LAWS OF THE LAND

When Ruth meets Boaz, he says to her, "Now, listen, my daughter, do not go to glean in another field or leave this one, but keep close to my young women. Let your eyes be on the field that they are reaping, and go after them. Have I not charged the young men not to touch you" (Ruth 2:8–9)?

We may note that Boaz calls her "daughter." The young men called her a "Moabite." In this one word, Boaz is intrinsically living by the ethic of the Torah. When she is called a Moabite, the underlying message is that one can do whatever they want with this foreigner, who speaks in a foreign accent. This is especially true if the person concerned is a woman, and more so if women in Moabite society were treated like sexual slaves. Boaz sets aside all these notions when he calls her "daughter." In ancient culture, the idea was, "You are my daughter, and I am going to make sure that you are treated like my daughter."

Following this he orders the young men not to touch her. The Hebrew, *naga'*, suggests a forceful, violent form of touching. This is a powerful ethical stance taken by a person who is seeking to live by the ethics of the Torah.

Ruth's response suggests that she is completely shocked by this response of Boaz. This was completely countercultural. She knelt before him with her forehead to the ground, and says, "Why have I found grace in your eyes, that you should take notice (*nakar*) of me? I am just a foreigner, (*nakari*)" (Ruth 2:10). The Hebrew text has an intentional play on words here. A *nakari* is a specific kind of foreign woman, she is one who is used as a sexual slave. A *nakar* person, quite in contrast to this, is a person of noteworthiness, usually a person from the landed class of society.

This interaction gives us another crucial #MeToo principle. The *nakari*, a foreign and vulnerable woman, must be transformed into the *nakar*, the notable woman, in order for injustice to be abolished. In this narrative, Boaz makes sure that refugee women are not merely given alms and made to feel beholden. Rather, he makes sure that they are transformed into noteworthy persons. This is a crucial strategy in overturning systems of injustice into systems of justice and righteousness.

Another reason behind Boaz's decision is seen in his response to Ruth. Most English translations translate, as in the NIV, "May the LORD repay you for what you have done. May you be richly rewarded by the LORD, the God of Israel, under whose wings you have come to take refuge" (Ruth 2:12 NIV). However, the word which is usually translated as "repay" (NIV, ESV), and "reward" (NRSV, TNK) is the Hebrew word *shalam,* which means to bring to a place of completeness and peacefulness. This is the goal of the biblical philosophy of justice. Boaz was in fact praying that Ruth would come to a place of complete wholeness and healing.

This is a crucial principle, because when women are abused they are completely destroyed psychologically, mentally, spiritually, and physically. Boaz's goal was to ensure a deep healing in the life of Ruth, or for that matter any other #MeToo woman.

In Boaz's reasoning we find another crucial verb *Chasah,* "to take refuge." This Hebrew verb has deep religious roots. In Egyptian and other ancient Near Eastern religions, when someone takes *chasah* in a deity, one commits herself fully into the service of that deity. In the case of women, this was usually the sexual cult (Deut 32:37; Isa 30:2; Ps 118:8–9). Instead of going this route, which was common in Moab, Ruth took "refuge" under the "wings" of YHWH, the God of Israel. This is a crucial point because later Ruth uses the same words when she proposes to Boaz in Ruth 3:9, "Spread your wings over your servant, because you are my kinsman redeemer." Boaz was supposed to be doing the same thing that God does to vulnerable women.

Then Boaz invites her to the Passover meal (Ruth 2:14). The Passover meal is the most poignant meal in the Jewish culture, then and now. It was the final meal of an enslaved community, a community that was brutally enslaved for 400 years. It remained the most important meal of the community so they would remember that they were enslaved once and therefore must never enslave anyone else. It reminded them, and still reminds them, of the faithfulness of God in delivering them from slavery. They remembered that the people who suffered the most during the Egyptian enslavement were women and girls. They remembered that the Egyptian tyrant king ordered the baby boys to be killed and baby girls to be kept alive, so that they would serve as sexual slaves. So when Boaz invited Ruth to the Passover meal, he was inviting her, a foreigner, to the most poignant meal of the Jewish community. It was saying to her, "We have suffered as well. Our women have suffered as well. Come participate in the remembrance of our suffering."

When Ruth takes the elements of the Passover meal to her mother-in-law, Naomi, she immediately knows that this person, Boaz, is genuine. So, she urges Ruth to propose to him. That is the story of Ruth chapter 3.

Naomi's wish for Ruth is seen in her introduction to the idea, "My daughter, should I not seek rest for you, that it may be good for you" (Ruth 3:1)? The ideas of "rest" and "good" are both from the creation narrative. God gave "rest" (*Nuach*) to the primeval human being in the garden of Eden (Gen 2:15). When he created everything, he created them to be "good" (Gen 1:4, 10, 12, 18, 21, 25, 31).

These two words, again, describe the antidote to all evil in society. The biblical answer is a return back to the ethics of the garden of Eden. It is an environment of rest (*Nuach*) and goodness (*Tov*). This is the goal of the biblical #MeToo movement.

WHAT ABOUT UNCOVERING FEET?

Naomi then advises Ruth,

> "Boaz, with whose women you have worked, is a relative of ours. Tonight he will be winnowing barley on the threshing floor. Wash, put on perfume, and get dressed in your best clothes. Then go down to the threshing floor, but don't let him know you are there until he has finished eating and drinking. When he lies down, note the place where he is lying. Then go and uncover his feet and lie down. He will tell you what to do."
>
> "I will do whatever you say," Ruth answered. So she went down to the threshing floor and did everything her mother-in-law told her to do. When Boaz had finished eating and drinking and was in good spirits, he went over to lie down at the far end of the grain pile. Ruth approached quietly, uncovered his feet and lay down. In the middle of the night something startled the man; he turned—and there was a woman lying at his feet! "Who are you?" he asked. "I am your servant Ruth," she said. "Spread the corner of your garment (Lit. spread you wings) over me, since you are a guardian-redeemer of our family." (Ruth 3:2–9 NIV)

It has been proposed by some modern interpreters that Ruth actually seduces Boaz, and that "uncovering the feet" is just a euphemism for a sexual encounter between Boaz and Ruth.[20] It seems to me that this interpretation does not go along with the rest of the narrative to Ruth. The straightforward interpretation of this narrative is that Ruth did precisely what Naomi, her mother-in-law, asked her to do. Naomi knew the cultural

20. E.g. Brenner, *Feminist Companion to Ruth*.

norms of Bethlehemite society. "Uncovering the feet" and asking Boaz to "spread your wings over me, since you are my Kinsman Redeemer" was an act of asking for a covenant, which he acknowledged she had already made with the God of the Bible (Ruth 2:12). This action of "spreading out wings" is essentially what God promised the Exodus community (Deut 32:11). This action of God is symbolized in the heart of the temple, where the cherubim also "spread out their wings" over the mercy seat (Exod 25:20; 37:9; 1 Kgs 6:27; 8:7). This is the action that Ruth is envisaging. According to Naomi's advice, she was simply asking a faithful man to follow through with the ethics of the Torah, regarding the duties of the *Goel*. The Passover narrative reminded the people that God himself was their *Goel*, who delivered them from slavery (Exod 6:6; 15:3). Therefore, the redeemed people were always asked to become *Goel* to others, especially close family members who fell into poverty, so that no one might fall into poverty in perpetuity, and so that no one would take advantage of the poor and the widow (Lev 25). These laws declare that in the Year of Jubilee, which happens every fiftieth year, all the property would return back to the original families. Anyone who is in debt is released from their debt. This would happen so that no family remains in poverty in perpetuity. The whole economy was supposed to return back to the ethos of Genesis 1.

The law of *Goel* was there to make sure that the poor family did not even need to wait for the Year of Jubilee. A *Goe'l*, or kinsman redeemer, could act on behalf of their generous God, pay off their debt, and buy off their land for them. It becomes clear that this was not happening during the time of the Judges. No wonder a Levite could own a sex slave. That was emblematic of the whole society.

My study of human trafficking across the globe makes it clear to me that financial debt is at the root of all sex trafficking. Debt bondage is the most-used ruse to control victims of labor and sex trafficking. Debts are multiplied on families through various petty and unjust rules. Then boys and girls are forced to pay off the debts accrued to their families by being sold into the sex industry. It is a multi-billion-dollar industry.

This was true in ancient times, as well.

Boaz's response is quite telling. He says,

> "The LORD bless you, my daughter," he replied. "This kindness is greater than that which you showed earlier: You have not run after the younger men, whether rich or poor. And now, my daughter, don't be afraid. I will do for you all you ask. All the people of

my town know that you are a woman of noble character. (Ruth 3:10–11 NIV)

Boaz describes her action, as an action of "grace" (*Chesed*). This is an action which is generally used of God (Exod 20:6; 34:6, 7; Deut 5:10), and in the narrative of Ruth itself it is used of God (Ruth 1:8; 2:20). In using this word, Ruth is being given a very high status in life. She is not merely a foreigner of whom anyone can take advantage. She is a woman of high status, who can bestow grace on others, like Boaz.

Boaz also acknowledges her with the highest status of womanhood. "All the chief justices, or people who sit at the city gate (*Sha'ar Ami*) know that you are an *Eshet Chayil*" (Ruth 3:11).

RUTH AMONG WISDOM LITERATURE: THE #METOO ESHET CHAYIL

In the Hebrew Bible, the book of Ruth does not follow the book of Judges, as is the case in English translations of the Bible. Those versions of the Bible follow the ordering of books as listed in the LXX, the Greek translation of the Bible. In the Hebrew Bible, the book of Ruth is part of five scrolls, or the *Megillot*, which follow the book of Proverbs. These are the books of Song of Songs, Ruth, Lamentations, Ecclesiastes, and Esther.

The book of Proverbs ends with an amazing poem regarding a woman. Most English translations characterize this woman with phrases like, "a capable wife" (NRSV), "excellent wife" (ESV), and "wife of noble character" (NIV) (all from Prov 31:10). The Hebrew phrase *"Eshet Chayil"* is the female counterpart of what Boaz is called in Ruth 2:1. He is called a *Chayil*. The NRSV translates this as "a prominent rich man", the NIV translates this as "a man of standing", and the ESV translates it as "a worthy man." One wonders why the woman of Proverbs 31:10 is not called "a prominent rich woman" or "a woman of standing" or "a worthy woman." Indeed, Ruth is called an *Eshet Chayil* twice in the book of Ruth. In Ruth 3:11, Boaz states that the chief justices of the people, who sit at the Gates, or the courts, know that she is an *Eshet Chayil*. In Ruth 4:11, this time all the elders of the city and the chief justices sing a song about Ruth:

> We are witnesses. May the LORD make the woman, who is coming into your house, like Rachel and Leah, who together built up

the house of Israel. May she be an *Eshet Chayil*[21] in Ephrathah and be renowned in Bethlehem."

The use of the phrase "*Eshet Chayil*" in the context of its use in the rest of the Bible suggests that it describes a physically, spiritually, mentally, emotionally, morally, ethically strong woman. It is not someone with whom others would try to mess around.

All five books of the *Megillot*, which follows the book of Proverbs, describe the characteristics of an *Eshet Chayil*. This is the biblical answer to injustice against women. It is to transform women into *Eshet Chayil*. Song of Songs deals with issues of women who are treated unjustly in an abusive relationship; Ruth deals with issues of women who are treated with gross injustice when they are widows and foreigners; Lamentations deals with injustices which are promulgated against a whole group of people when the whole city or country cries out in pain because of enslavement; Ecclesiastes deals with injustices that are done to the elderly, especially elderly women; and Esther deals with the problem of racial injustice, which leads to genocide.

I will deal with the other four *Megillot* in a a book which I intend to write.

In the following, I would like to show how making Ruth an *Eshet Chayil* furthers the biblical answer to the issues raised by the #MeToo movement.

BOAZ THE REDEEMER AND RUTH THE ESHET CHAYIL

In the story of Ruth, Boaz is constantly called the "redeemer" (*Go'el*), since he "redeems" (*Ga'al*; Ruth 2:20; 3:9, 12, 13; 4:1, 3, 4, 6, 7, 8, 14). In the Torah, God is called the Redeemer. He is the one who redeems from evil, (Gen 48:16), as well as from horrible persecution and slavery (Exod 6:6; 15:13). The prophets and kings also acknowledge God to be the Redeemer (2 Sam 4:9; 7:23; 1 Kgs 1:29). In his deep suffering, Job constantly looks to God to be his redeemer who will ultimately heal him from this suffering. Job exclaims, "I know that my redeemer lives, and at last he will stand upon the earth" (Job 19:25; 5:20; 6:23; 33:28). God is constantly called Redeemer in the Psalms of Lament (Ps 25:22; 26:11; 69:18, and so on). These are Psalms

---

21. The NRSV translates this Hebrew phrase as, "may you produce children"; the NIV translates it as, "may you have a standing"; and the ESV translates it as "may you act worthily."

43

which enable the worshipper to face persecution and suffering at the hands of evil people.

This is the model that God expected his redeemed to follow. They in turn had to be redeemers of others. This is reflected in all the laws related to redemption, which we enumerated in the last section. The redeemed people of God were supposed to redeem the people who were physically, socially, politically marginalized. The prophet Isaiah says that "redeeming" is synonymous with "recreating" (Isa 43:1; 44:24). The prophet Jeremiah declares that the purpose of the act of redemption is to deliver others from evil and ruthless people (Jer 15:21).

This was the commission given to God's people, and is an important answer to the issues raised by the #MeToo movement. Sadly, only Boaz is shown as fulfilling this redemptive commission.

Ruth 3 and 4 set out the drama of redemption. The questions that are posed in the narrative that follows are, "Who is the real example of a human redeemer? Who follows God's model?" There was another prospective redeemer who was closer in line to redeem Naomi and Ruth. This person was to be given the first opportunity to redeem them. So, in keeping with the protocol of that time, Boaz brought this person before the city gate, the Supreme Court of that time. The English translation of Ruth 4:1 reads, "Boaz said, 'Come over here, my friend, and sit down'" (Ruth 4:1 NIV, NRSV, and ESV). The Hebrew just says, "Come over here, and sit down, so and so, so and so, (peloni almoni)." This is not a phrase one used for a friend. It is more appropriate to interpret this as used of a nondescript individual. He just did everything that society around him did, especially in how they treated women and the marginalized.

Boaz takes this person to the city gate, and lays before him the first proposition, the economic aspect of redemption. He says to him:

> "Naomi, who has come back from the country of Moab, is selling the parcel of land that belonged to our kinsman Elimelech. So, I thought I would tell you of it, and say: Buy it in the presence of those sitting here, and in the presence of the elders of my people. If you will redeem it, redeem it; but if you will not, tell me, so that I may know; for there is no one prior to you to redeem it, and I come after you." So he said, "I will redeem it." (Ruth 4:3–4 NRSV)

This economic proposition of redemption is based on Lev 25. The underlying principle is Lev 25:23. In this the LORD who delivered the people from slavery and gave them the promised land gives them the following law, "The land shall not be sold in perpetuity, for the land is mine. For you are strangers and sojourners with me. In all the land you possess, you shall practice the principle of redemption (*Ge-ulah*) of the land." This principle required the people to always be cognizant of the fact that they were slaves, and that this land was given to them as a gift by God. They had to always keep in mind that their identity was always that of being "strangers and sojourners," just like their forefathers Abraham, Isaac, and Jacob. This perpetual identity characteristic would always ensure that they were just to "strangers and sojourners," especially women.

This central principle states that the "land belongs only to the LORD." It does not belong to individuals. Individuals were caretakers and stewards of the land, so that it is always used for God's good purposes. When the owner of a property keeps this in mind, then that person will never be puffed up to consider himself to be in a place to show contempt to the poor and marginalized.

Based on this central principle, the law of redemption goes on to state, "If your brother goes into a state of depression (*mukh)* and sells his inheritance (*achuzah*) then his nearest redeemer (*Goel*) shall come and redeem what his brother has sold" (Lev 25:25).

We must point out the Hebrew word which is usually translated as "becomes poor" (NIV and ESV) is essentially a state of poverty that happens as a result of social status, mental illness, physical disability, and any one of a whole range of disabilities of this sort. When misfortunes of this sort happened, it was the responsibility of the nearest *Goel* to redress the situation. This could take the form of buying back the property, but is not limited to that. It could be a whole range of measures the *Goel* must take to make sure that the person who is in a state of *mukh* is not in a place where others would take advantage of the person.

The Ruth narrative makes it clear that this unmentionable *Goel* was willing to do only the basic minimum. He was willing to buy back the property.

After Boaz had cleared the first proposition, he proceeded to the next proposition. He said, "On the day you buy the land from Naomi, you also acquire Ruth the Moabite, the dead man's widow, in order to maintain the name of the dead with his property" (Ruth 4:5 NIV). This proposition is based on Deuteronomy 25:5–10, generally called the law of Levirate marriage. This law requires that if a person dies, then it was the legal duty of the nearest relative/brother to marry the woman. The word Levirate derives from the Latin, *levir*, which refers to the husband's brother. This law is preceded by the reminder, "remember that you were slaves in the land of Egypt" (Deut 24:22). In light of this, they were required to take care of the "immigrants, women and widows" (Deut 24:19). These laws were supposed to be foremost in the minds of the Israelites during the wheat and the barley harvest times, i.e., the time between Passover and Pentecost.

Widows in ancient Near Eastern societies, as in many societies today—like India, for example—have a very bad place in society. In ancient Near Eastern religions, widows were supposed to be living the lives of temple prostitutes, (*Qadesha*). They were forced to do this to pay off the debts of the family when they fell into poverty and sold off their land. Ancient Near Eastern religions took further advantage of the misfortune of widows, and used the income they earned to finance the temples.

The Bible, in contrast to this evil practice, gave the widow a position of strength and security. She had the right to be married to her husband's brother, or the nearest relative. We encountered the full intensity of this law in the Judah and Tamar narrative. Tamar herself took matters into her own hands. In response, Judah was forced to admit, "She is more just (*Tsadiqah*) than I, because I did not give Shelah my son to her" (Gen 38:26).

Boaz is shown here as the anti-Judah. Further, Boaz is portrayed as a good interpreter of the Torah. The ongoing dialogue at the city gate shows a very important interpretive principle. It is called the principle of inner-biblical intertextuality. This interpretive principle shows that the laws of the Bible are interdependent on each other and cannot be practiced in isolation. In this case, the Ruth narrative shows that laws regarding *mukh*, or poverty resulting from any kind of handicap—including widowhood—must be practiced interdependently with other laws. Widowhood was a huge handicap in world society then, just as it is now.

The economic law of redemption, with respect to widows, gives the principle that no widow shall be left without her property. The social law of Levirate marriage dictated that all widows had the right to get married to the next of kin of her deceased husband. Both laws were to protect the widow, so that evil people would not take advantage of them.

Keeping in mind this intertextuality of biblical laws, Boaz says, "On the day you buy the land from Naomi, you also acquire Ruth the Moabite, the dead man's widow, in order to maintain the name of the dead with his property" (Ruth 4:5 NIV).

In response to this, the nondescript redeemer said, "Then I cannot redeem it because I might endanger my own estate. You redeem it yourself. I cannot do it" (Ruth 4:6 NIV).

Obviously, this so-and-so redeemer did not understand the underlying principles behind the two laws. He was willing to buy the property and give it to Naomi out of his riches. That did not impact him in the slightest bit. However, getting married to a widow—a low-level immigrant foreigner no less—that was something else. That would endanger his place in society, and he did not want to take that risk.

The Ruth narrative seeks to make it clear that engagement with issues of systemic injustice against women cannot be a hands-off approach, or merely an economic approach. It has to be a holistic approach, and must include a deep personal involvement. Only this kind of approach can solve problems of injustices against women in global society.

There is another underlying and very crucial principle behind the biblical *modus operandi* of dealing with issues of the #MeToo movement. This principle, sadly, is lost in the translation into English. The English translation reads as follows:

> I thought I should bring the matter to your attention and suggest that you *buy* it in the presence of these seated here and in the presence of the elders of my people.
>
> Then Boaz said, "On the day you *buy* (*acquire*, NRSV) the land from Naomi, you also *acquire* Ruth the Moabite, the dead man's widow.
>
> So, the guardian-redeemer said to Boaz, "*Buy* (NRSV, acquire) it yourself." And he removed his sandal.
>
> Then Boaz announced to the elders and all the people, "Today you are witnesses that I have *bought* (NRSV, acquired) from Naomi all the property of Elimelek, Kilion and Mahlon. I have also acquired (NRSV) Ruth the Moabite, Mahlon's widow, as my wife." (Ruth 4:4–10 NIV)

To begin with, in the above dialogue, the word which is translated as "bought" and "acquired" in prominent English language translations, is a very derogatory term. It is odd that the English translations would portray a woman as being "bought" or "acquired." It goes against the whole ethos of womanhood and marriage in the Bible. It also plays into the hands of ancient Near Eastern religions, where that is how women were treated. They were treated as the property of men, who could do whatever they wanted with them.

47

The Hebrew word used here is a very strong one. It is used of God in a crucial text of the Torah, where Melchizedek, "the just king," the King of Salem, "Peace," blessed Abram. He said to him, "Blessed be Abram of God Most High, Creator (*qanah*) of heaven and earth" (Gen 14:19, 22). After the Lord rescued the people from slavery in Egypt, he took them through the Sea of Reeds or Red Sea. The Song of Moses and Miriam, which is sung right after the recreation event through the Red Sea, expresses this in a crucial refrain, "Till your people, Passover, O LORD; till the people, Passover, the people you have created (*qanah*)" (Lev 25:14, 15, 44). Similarly, this Hebrew word is used constantly in the context of the Year of Jubilee text in Lev 25, which describes the *qanah*, or recreation of a new society and economy (Lev 25:14, 15, 44, 45). In Deuteronomy, Moses reminds the second generation of the people, the Lord is the one, "who created (*qanah*) you, who made (*asah*) you, and who established you" (Deut 32:6).

This theme is repeated numerous times in the worship songs of Israel. Psalm 139:13 exults, "For you created (*qanah*) my inward parts; you knitted me together in my mother's womb." Remembering the Exodus event again, Psalm 78:54 rejoices, "He brought them to his holy land; to the mountain which his right hand created (*qanah*)."

These and other texts from the Hebrew Bible make it clear that the Bible expects radical, deep, and lasting solutions to the question of evil and injustice in society.

Boaz is not merely asking to buy or acquire the land. The word used in these verses is *qanah*. He is asking for the "recreation" of a new economy. He is not asking for the "acquiring" of Ruth, as the English translations sadly put it. He is asking for the recreation of a new person.

Boaz is saying:

> I thought I should bring the matter to your attention and suggest that you *recreate* (*qanah*) it in the presence of these seated here and in the presence of the elders of my people.
>
> Then Boaz said, "On the day you *recreate* (*qanah*) the land from Naomi, you also *recreate* Ruth the Moabite, the dead man's widow" . . . So, the redeemer person said to Boaz, "*recreate* it yourself." And he removed his sandal.
>
> Then Boaz announced to the elders and all the people, "Today you are witnesses that I have *recreated* for Naomi all the property of Elimelek, Kilion and Mahlon. I have also *recreated* Ruth the Moabite, Mahlon's widow, as my wife. (Ruth 4:4, 5, 8, 9, 10, my translation)

48

Ruth is a woman who must have seen so much pain in her child-hood, given the makeup of Moabite religions. This is a person who was used as a prostitute by her own husband. This husband, it should be noted, was himself an immigrant refugee. Yet he took advantage of the women of Moab just because that is how women were treated in Moabite society. This husband should have been conversant with the laws of the Torah, but instead he did what was the easiest thing to do. This woman's identity was completely shattered. Then this shattered woman becomes an immigrant refugee in a foreign land. She leaves the familiar environment of Moab to go to the complete unknown of Bethlehem. Thankfully, she has another woman, Naomi, whose life and faithfulness she has observed carefully. So, she says to her, "Your God will be my God; your people my people; I am going to stick with you till death do us part" (Ruth 1:16–17).

Thankfully, she encounters a person, Boaz, who lives by the ethics of the Torah. These ethics have a very high order. The laws of the Torah can-not stand any injustice and evil. The Torah's response to injustice and evil is not merely a Band-Aid treatment, here and there. Those are thin ethical responses to the problem of evil. The Torah's response is a thick ethical response to the problem of evil against women. It is the recreation of a new economy. It is the recreation of a new society. It is the recreation of a new woman, beginning with Ruth the Moabitess.

There is a complete change in Bethlehemite society that day. A revival. A resurgence.

As soon as Boaz makes this radical proclamation, then all the people who are at the gate, along with the elders, say, "We are witnesses. May the LORD make the woman who is coming into your house like Rachel and Leah, who together built up the house of Israel. May you produce children in Ephrathah and bestow a name in Bethlehem" (Ruth 4:11 NRSV).

In the Hebrew sentence structure, the first people to recognize this amazing transformation were the common people (*'am Ha-aretz*). This was then followed by the elders. It is crucial to note this sequence. In the Bible, any radical and lasting transformation begins with the common people, not with the leaders. This is very different from the other societies which surrounded Israel. Why would the king and the religious leaders of ancient Near Eastern society want transformation? They were quite comfortable in life, even though injustices around them were very clearly evident. They were very glad to abuse the poor and women.

It is clear that the Ruth narrative wants the reader to see that Boaz's act of faithfulness to the Torah, and the God of the Torah, gave the common people the courage to take the lead in countering evil. The lead of the common people was then followed by the elders. In many ways this is also true to issues that have been raised by the #MeToo movement. One of the drawbacks of the #MeToo movement is that it begins with women who are prominent already. They are heard, because they are prominent in society.

A key principle of the #MeToo movement in the Ruth narrative is that it begins with a woman who is an unknown person. It spreads through the low classes of society and then reaches the upper echelons of society.

A principle which emerges from this action of Boaz is that when one confronts evil and injustice, one must not only go to the politicians, judges, and the leaders of society. One must follow the wise example of Boaz, and take the common human beings along.

Sadly, the voice of the common woman is still not heard in much of the world. I read stories from India, Pakistan, Bangladesh, Myanmar, Egypt, Congo, and Kenya (among many others), of women who are abused and raped. Sadly, no one hears their stories. They are considered to be *persona non-grata*.

The #MeToo movement of the Bible urges us to reach out to those Ruths in the global society today.

The proclamation led by the common people gave Ruth equality with the founding mothers of the nation: Rachel and Leah. She is also called the *Eshet Chayil*, the amazing Wonder Woman of Proverbs 31.

Ruth indeed becomes the matriarch of the Messiah, in the line of two previous #MeToo matriarchs—Tamar and Rahab—who were also destroyed and raped by society. However, they also were *recreated* into new women—*Eshet Chayil*, Wonder Women.

5

The Wife of Uriah and the #MeToo Movement

The fourth woman who is highlighted in the genealogy of Jesus the Messiah is not even mentioned by name. The NIV translates the Greek as follows: "David was the father of Solomon, whose mother had been Uriah's wife" (Matt 1:6 NIV). The NRSV has it right when it says, "And David was the father of Solomon by the wife of Uriah" (Matt 1:6 NRSV). In this crucial section, Matthew's Gospel is making it clear that Bathsheba was not the wife of David. She was the wife of Uriah, a Hittite, a minority who was forced to serve in the military of King David. Yet he served David with complete faithfulness. Bathsheba herself was a foreigner, a Gilonite just like Tamar, Rahab, and Ruth.

THE NARRATIVE OF RUTH AND BATHSHEBA, IN 2 SAMUEL 11–12.

In the Hebrew Bible, the books Joshua, Judges, 1 and 2 Samuel, and 1 and 2 Kings are not called historical books. They are called the books of the Prophets and are considered to be a prophetic evaluation of the lives of the judges and kings. In the Bible, the kings are not considered to be at the top of society since prophets are considered to be higher than kings. They are the ones who write down the evaluations of the kings, which becomes prophetic history. This is quite different from the kings of other nations. Those kings were regarded as the divine beings, gods who should be worshipped. In Israelite history, quite in contrast to this politic, kings were subject to the prophets and the Torah.

These prophetic history books are also called Deuteronomist history. A crucial text is found in the book of Deuteronomy, which underscores the relationship between kings and prophets. Deuteronomy 17:14–20 lays out the meaning of kingship in the context of Israel. For one thing, the people are told that this king should not be as the kings of the other nations. The kings of the Sumerians, Egyptians, etc. were considered divine beings, and the horses they had were symbols of their divine power. The people of Israel were told that the power of the Israelite kings should not reside in religious powers like divine horses. Nor must the kings of Israel seek to acquire queens, like the Sumerians and the Egyptians. The queens of these people groups were considered to be goddesses, who used their divine powers to subjugate people.

To make sure that the kings and queens of Israel did not become like the kings and queens of the people groups around them, the Israelite second Exodus generation were given the following injunction:

> "When he takes the throne of his kingdom, he is to write for himself on a scroll a copy of this Torah, taken from that of the Levitical priests. It is to be with him, and he is to read it all the days of his life so that he may learn to revere the LORD his God and follow carefully all the words of this law and these decrees and not consider himself better than his fellow Israelites and turn from the law to the right or to the left. Then he and his descendants will reign a long time over his kingdom in Israel." (Deut 17:18–20 NIV)

Before the king took on his responsibility of kingship, he had to write for himself every word of the Torah on a scroll. This was a tedious task. Yet, it was a task which reminded him that his rule was to be under the authority of the Torah. He had to read from it every day of his kingship (Deut 17:14–20). His laws, his judgments, the day-to-day affairs, etc., all of this was supposed to be subject to the Torah. The Torah was the great equalizer. Both the common people and the king were subject to the Torah, and the God of the Torah. This would keep the king from doing unjust things to his subjects.

The Levites were responsible for making sure the Torah was transmitted accurately, and interpreted rightly. The prophets were responsible for making sure that the king and the society carried out the laws and the ethos of the Torah in society.

Did the kings of Israel and Judah stick with this injunction?

There is no indication that the kings wrote for themselves a copy of the Torah. There is one instance where a teenage king by the name of Josiah got the temple cleaned up, and during this process, the priests found a copy of the Torah. When it was read to king Josiah, he realized that the people of his kingdom had done much evil and had stood against the precepts of the Torah, so he declared a fast of repentance, which led to an ethical and moral revival in the whole community (2 Kings 22). On another occasion, there was a public reading of the Torah during the postexilic time of the prophets Ezra and Nehemiah (Neh 7–8) which resulted in a great systemic cleansing of the society and renewal of the ethics of society.

WHY DID THE RAPE OF THE WIFE OF URIAH HAPPEN?

The story of David and Bathsheba is found primarily in 2 Samuel 11–12. First Chronicles 20:1 merely mentions, "In the spring of the year, the time when kings go out to battle, Joab led out the army and ravaged the country of the Ammonites and came and besieged Rabbah. But David remained at Jerusalem." It is as if the Chronicler is reluctant to go into the details of this awful event. However, we may note two aspects of narrative which are common to the two accounts. These two things hold the key to a downward slide in David's ethics. Before this time, David was a very ethical person. He was a shepherd who was chosen to be a king (1 Sam 16), and then he kills the divine king Goliath (1 Sam 17). In the following chapters, Saul constantly seeks to kill him. On several occasions, David could have killed Saul, but because of his strong ethical character he does not do so. In fact, in 2 Samuel 1, he bitterly mourns the death of Saul. In 2 Samuel 7, Nathan the prophet prophesies concerning David's dynasty. It is generally called the Davidic covenant. The Davidic covenant has the following ingredients. It should be noted that each of these ingredients is patterned after the Abrahamic (Father of the nation) covenant (Gen 12, 15, 17):

1. David is promised "a great name," (2 Sam 7:9), in whom all the families of the earth will be blessed.

2. He is promised the place of encounter, where people will encounter God (2 Sam 7:10).

3. He is promised a "messianic rest" (2 Sam 7:11).

4. He is promised a "messianic seed" (2 Sam 7:12).

5. He is promised an everlasting kingdom (2 Sam 7:13).

6. He is promised a person who will be the eternal Son (2 Sam 7:14).

7. He is promised that this will be the Torah, the code of ethics for all humanity (2 Sam 7:19).

This is a great universal commission which is given to David and his dynasty.

Things were going quite well for David. God had made promises to him, including that his kingdom would not merely be a Jewish kingdom and that through his seed, the Messiah would come and his eternal kingdom would be one for all of humanity.

So, what happened to David? What caused him to commit the heinous rape of Bathsheba?

The simple storyline goes as follows, as it is translated in the NIV:

2 SAMUEL 11

In the spring, at the time when kings go off to war, David sent Joab out with the king's men and the whole Israelite army. They destroyed the Ammonites and besieged Rabbah. But David remained in Jerusalem. One evening David got up from his bed and walked around on the roof of the palace. From the roof, he saw a woman bathing. The woman was very beautiful, and David sent someone to find out about her. The man said, "She is Bathsheba, the daughter of Eliam and the wife of Uriah the Hittite." Then David sent messengers to get her. She came to him, and he slept with her. (Now she was purifying herself from her monthly uncleanness.) Then she went back home. The woman conceived and sent word to David, saying, "I am pregnant."

So, David sent this word to Joab: "Send me Uriah the Hittite." And Joab sent him to David. When Uriah came to him, David asked him how Joab was, how the soldiers were and how the war was going. Then David said to Uriah, "Go down to your house and wash your feet." So, Uriah left the palace, and a gift from the king was sent after him. But Uriah slept at the entrance to the palace with all his master's servants and did not go down to his house. David was told, "Uriah did not go home." So, he asked Uriah,

"Haven't you just come from a military campaign? Why didn't you go home?" Uriah said to David, "The ark and Israel and Judah are staying in tents, and my commander Joab and my lord's men are camped in the open country. How could I go to my house to eat and drink and make love to my wife? As surely as you live, I will not do such a thing!" Then David said to him, "Stay here one more day, and tomorrow I will send you back." So, Uriah remained in Jerusalem that day and the next. At David's invitation, he ate and drank with him, and David made him drunk. But in the evening Uriah went out to sleep on his mat among his master's servants; he did not go home.

In the morning, David wrote a letter to Joab and sent it with Uriah. In it he wrote, "Put Uriah out in front where the fighting is fiercest. Then withdraw from him so he will be struck down and die." So, while Joab had the city under siege, he put Uriah at a place where he knew the strongest defenders were. When the men of the city came out and fought against Joab, some of the men in David's army fell; moreover, Uriah the Hittite died. Joab sent David a full account of the battle. He instructed the messenger: "When you have finished giving the king this account of the battle, the king's anger may flare up, and he may ask you, 'Why did you get so close to the city to fight? Didn't you know they would shoot arrows from the wall? Who killed Abimelech, son of Jerub-Besheth? Didn't a woman drop an upper millstone on him from the wall, so that he died in Thebez? Why did you get so close to the wall?' If he asks you this, then say to him, 'Moreover, your servant Uriah the Hittite is dead.'"

The messenger set out, and when he arrived he told David everything Joab had sent him to say. The messenger said to David, "The men overpowered us and came out against us in the open, but we drove them back to the entrance of the city gate. Then the archers shot arrows at your servants from the wall, and some of the king's men died. Moreover, your servant Uriah the Hittite is dead." David told the messenger, "Say this to Joab: 'Don't let this upset you; the sword devours one as well as another. Press the attack against the city and destroy it.' Say this to encourage Joab."

When Uriah's wife heard that her husband was dead, she mourned for him. After the time of mourning was over, David had her brought to his house, and she became his wife and bore him a son. But the thing David had done displeased the LORD. (2 Sam 11:1–27 NIV)

It should be noted that what happed is described in the conclusion of this narrative in the strongest language possible. The NIV above translates it as, "The thing David had done displeased the LORD." This is a severe understatement. The literal Hebrew should translate, "The word (*Davar*), i.e. the very philosophical basis behind what David did, was EVIL in the eyes of the LORD." I have capitalized the word evil, because that is the emphasis of the Hebrew sentence.

Further, it would be good to note the difference between how this horrible event is described in 2 Samuel and 1 Chronicles. The history of the kings is described in two sets of materials. On one hand, it is found in what scholars call the Deuteronomist history. The Hebrew Bible simply called this prophetic history. These are the books of Joshua, Judges, 1 and 2 Samuel, and 1 and 2 Kgs. These give us the prophetic evaluation of the reign of the kings. It should be noted that that is what history is. History is the evaluation of events. Prophetic history is the prophetic evaluation of the lives of the kings. Unfortunately, for most of the kings, the prophetic analysis concludes with the words, "So and so king did evil, (*ra'*) in the eyes of the LORD. (1 Kgs 11:6; 13:33; 14:22; 15:26, and so on).

The books of the Chronicles give a different kind of analysis of the live of the kings. These give us a postexilic (after the exile) account of the reign of the kings. The comparative study of these two sets of accounts is called Synoptic analysis. This kind of a study yields some very good conclusions and biblical theology. In the New Testament, this kind of a study is done when comparing how Jesus' life and teachings are presented in the Gospels of Matthew, Mark, and Luke. These are called the Synoptic Gospels.

The Chronicler's description of the kings is more succinct, and invites a wisdom analysis of the lives of the kings.

In the case of the David and Bathsheba narrative, 1 Chronicles 20 does not give many of the details which are found in 2 Samuel 11–12, and yet its brevity carries a lot of force.

The Chronicler's account reads as follows:

> In the spring, at the time when kings go off to war, Joab led out the armed forces. He laid waste the land of the Ammonites and went to Rabbah and besieged it, but David remained in Jerusalem. (1 Chr 20:1 NIV)

This brief description is followed by how David enslaved the people, and made them do forced labor quite similar to what the king of Egypt did to the children of Israel (1 Chr 20:2, 3).

THE PRACTICE OF ANCIENT NEAR EASTERN RITUAL SEX WITH WOMEN UNDER TREES BEFORE WARS

There are two common themes underlined between the two reports. One is that the incident happened during the springtime. Literally, "during the yearly time of return or repentance" (*LeTashivath Hashanah*, 2 Sam 11:1; 1 Chr 20:1). Most English translations suggest that this is "springtime of the year" (the NIV, NRSV, etc.). This translation captures one aspect of the phrase, *LeTashivath Hashnah*, i.e., it is the time of the turn of the year, which is springtime. However, readers of the original Hebrew would know that this season was the Passover season, the beginning of the new biblical year, but more importantly, it was the time of the remembrance of God's salvation of an enslaved people from Egypt. In light of this, the people had to repent of all their wrongdoings against the poor, widows, orphans, aliens, and marginalized people. The narrative seeks to show that David did not spend his time reflecting on his life and rulership in the light of Passover repentance. On the contrary, he enslaved and used as forced labor the people his army defeated in battle.

Both the narratives also emphasize another aspect of this time of the year, and this is from a global perspective. This is the time when kings of the ancient Near East go to war. They go to war after they participate in religious rituals during the springtime, which empower them to defeat their enemies. What are these religious rituals?

Ancient Near Eastern texts give us much material to explore the background behind the David and Bathsheba narrative. One such story is that of the Sumerian goddess Inanna. She is the goddess of love, sexuality, and war. She is worshipped under the sacred fig tree. In Akkadian texts, she is called Ishtar. She is the daughter of Nanna, the moon god, and Ningal. She is the sister of the god Utu. According to ancient Near Eastern religions, the divine king derives power and sacred knowledge from drinking the intoxicating drink of the sacred fig tree. So does Inanna, his consort. This is commemorated by divine kings of the ancient Near East. Before they go to war, they have sex with priestesses of Inanna in a sacred ritual. One of the places where this ritual is described is in the famous Epic of Gilgamesh, tablet 12, "The Huluppu Tree." In this ritual poem, Inanna finds and nurtures the huluppu tree. However, the serpent god opposes her. Gilgamesh comes to the rescue of the tree and saves it from other gods. As the story goes on, Gilgamesh encourages her to marry Dumuzid, the shepherd god.

However, that is not in Inanna's purpose. She makes love to all the king-gods who come to worship her, and so gives them her power.

These kinds of rituals are also found in other ancient Near Eastern religions. Springtime is associated with fertility rituals with the god Baal, and his consort/sister/wife Anat. Through a sexual orgy, Anat brings the dead Baal back to life; this is seen in the world as "spring." In Ugaritic religions, Anat is also depicted as a warrior goddess. She is depicted in one text (KTU 1.3 ii:3–30) as a bloodthirsty goddess who wades thigh-deep in the blood of the slain foes. Baal can only defeat his foes by the power that he gets from his sexual encounter with Anat. In Egyptian religion as well, Anat is called "the consort of kings, and the consort of dominions" (KTU 1.108 6–7).

Asherah is another consort/wife/mother of Baal. She bears him "seventy sons (gods)," (KTU 1.4 vi:46) so she is regarded as the mother of all gods. In Sumerian texts from the time of Hammurabi (18th century BC), she is called the "goddess of voluptuousness" (BM 22454)[22].

In keeping with these kinds of myths, ancient Near Eastern kings practice this sexual ritual during springtime with temple priestesses who perform the roles of Anat and Asherah.

In light of this bizarre ancient Near Eastern background, the Torah and the Prophets constantly warn the people against practicing these kinds of rituals. In the context of laying out the laws regarding the Feasts of the LORD, Deuteronomy 16 goes on to require that, "Justice be not perverted . . . Justice, only justice, you shall follow, that you may live and inherit the land which the LORD your God is giving you" (Deut 16:19–20). This injunction is immediately followed by, "You shall not plant any tree as an Asherah beside the altar of the LORD . . . You must not erect a pillar, which the LORD your God detests" (Deut 16:21–22). It is clear from the perspective of the Torah and the Prophets that these religious practices always lead to injustices against the poor and the marginalized. So the Torah strictly forbids these religious practices, which were very common in the ancient Near East. Sadly, the history of the children of Israel makes it clear that the worship of Baal and Asherah became a common practice very early on, as is clear from Judges 6.

The second aspect of the incident which is underlined by both the 2 Samuel 11 and 1 Chronicles 20 narratives is that David sat in Jerusalem.

---

22. BM is Ancient Near Eastern tablets in the collection of the British Museum. See, van der Toorn et al., *Dictionary of Deities and Demons*, 101.

The obvious question is, "Why is David remaining, literally sitting in Jerusalem?"

This is the question that the 2 Samuel 11 narrative seeks to answer.

It begins with describing that the incident happened in the evening. The original readers of the Bible would know that this was a bad sign. Sexual rituals happened at dusk, or "the time of the evening (*'et ha-erev*)." It must be noted in response to this that the Torah prescribes this time to be the crucial time of the evening sacrifices, e.g. the Passover Lamb (Exod 12:6; 23:5; Num 9:5; cf. Exod 29:39, 41; Num 28:8). It seems clear that the narrative is suggesting that instead of following the practice of celebrating the Passover during this springtime of the year, King David was about to venture into practices which were carried out by kings of other ancient Near Eastern societies.

Why would David see a woman bathing from his rooftop? This was what the kings of the ancient Near East did. The women who were treated as temple priestesses in the Inanna temple or the Baal/Anat/Asherah temple, etc. were available to the kings for sexual ritual at all times.

The actions of David were actions of movements toward a sexual ritual in ancient Near Eastern thought: "arising from his bed, walking, checking out" (2 Sam 11:2) the temple priestesses. He then sees a woman "washing" (*Rachatz*). In the Hebrew Bible, this is always act of cleansing seven days after the menstrual period of five days. This twelve-day period is called *niddah*. After this time, a woman would generally go through ritual cleansing, and this is what presumably, Bathsheba was doing (Lev 15:19–33). According to the narrative, David "saw" that "the woman was very beautiful" (2 Sam 11:2 NIV, NRSV). The Hebrew literally says, "He saw, she was very good." This reaction of David to the sight of Bathsheba is the same as God's reaction to all of creation: "And God saw everything he had made, and it was very good" (Gen 1:31). In using these words, in some sense, just like kings of the ancient Near East, David is regarding himself as divine. This is slipping further into dangerous territory.

When David sends his people to inquire about who the woman is, they report back to him that she is a foreigner. She is married to a Hittite by the name of Uriah. This should have been sufficient information for him not to make any bad decisions. However, sadly, David was bent on doing what the divine-kings of the ancient Near East did. Besides, she was a foreigner and he, as the king, could do whatever he desired.

David then sends his people and forcibly takes her. The verbal structure of this word is always used of the violent and forcible taking of a person or something (Gen 38:2; 1 Sam 15:21; 2 Sam 3:15; and so on). Then he has sexual intercourse with her. The verb which is used to describe this sexual encounter is always used of someone who has illicit and forcible sex with another person (Gen 19:32, 35; Deut 22:23, 25, 28). The usual word, which is used when speaking of a man having a sexual encounter with his wife, is a beautiful word. It is used, for example, of Adam and Eve : "Adam knew (*yada'*) his wife, and she conceived" (Gen 4:1, 17, 25, and so on).

The English translations miss the gravity of what David did. This was rape of a woman who belonged to a weaker section of society. She was a foreigner, and David knew that he could take advantage of the weak and the vulnerable anytime he wanted. He was the king, and all the kings of the world around him treated their subjects as their slaves. The act was given religious sanction, so David took advantage of the whole thing.

The woman returns to her home and in time finds out she is pregnant. She sends word to David and his immediate response is to somehow work it out that she would have sex with her husband. So, he sends for her husband, Uriah the Hittite. The narrative seeks to emphasize this. It is showing deep disdain for a minority community. When Uriah comes to David, the latter first engages in small talk, enquiring about the health and well-being of Joab, the commander-in-chief, and the rest of the army, and so on. The narrative shows sheer hypocrisy on the part of David. Then without any shame and with a wink in his eyes, he asks Uriah to go home and have sex with his wife. The Hebrew says, "wash your foot," which is euphemism for having sex. When David sends him on his way, very intentionally, he also sends for him a *mas'et*. This is no ordinary present or gift, as is translated in most English translations. It is used of religious offerings (Ezek 20:40; Amos 5:11). It is related to the word *nasa'*, a word used to subjugate women to religiously oriented sexual servitude. David was giving Uriah the money to buy his wife as a sexual slave. This is very disgusting.

Uriah does not go home, most certainly going through a range of emotions. For inexplicable reasons, he is brought back from the battlefield. His mind is still with his comrades, who are dying. It is Passover time. And then he receives this horrible "gift" from the king himself.

He sleeps with the "servants of the Lord," at the door of the palace, and word of this comes to David. So Uriah is called before David again, and the King says to him, "What is this I am hearing about you? Why have you not gone down to your house" (2 Sam 11:11)? Uriah responds with the following profound words:

"The ark and Israel and Judah are staying in tents, and my commander Joab and my lord's men are camped in the open country. How could I go to my house to eat and drink and make love to my wife? As surely as you live, I will not do such a thing" (2 Sam 11:11 NIV)!

These words are pregnant with an amazing expression of theology and faith. While the king himself was "sitting" (*Yashav*, 2 Sam 11:1; 1 Chr 20:1) in Jerusalem, the presence of God, as seen in the Ark, and all the people of Israel and Judah, were "sitting" (*yashav*) in booths (*sukkoth*). Living in *Sukkoth* was a crucial symbol of God's care for the people in the wilderness, when he took them out of Egypt during this springtime season of Passover (Lev 23:42, 43; Neh 8:14–17). This was the time when Moses and Joshua experienced the closest relationship with the God who saved them from the gods, and the divine king of Egypt.

The narrative seeks to show us the utter contrast between religious hypocrisy, utter disregard for the God of the Bible by King David, and the beautiful faith of a low-class Hittite. Right in the face of injustice, especially knowing that his wife was used as a religious prostitute! This is amazing!

Sadly, David does not get it. When he speaks to Uriah, he uses the same word which was used to describe his state of being, "he sat (*yashav*) in Jerusalem." He says, "Sit here (*yashav*) today, and tomorrow I will send you back. So, Uriah sat (*yashav*) in Jerusalem that day and the next (1 Sam 11:12).

What does "sitting" in Jerusalem mean? David gets drunk and he gets Uriah drunk as well. David is hoping that in a state of drunkenness, he will go and sleep with Bathsheba. But Uriah does not do that. In "the evening," the same time that David had raped his wife, after he got up from "his bed," (2 Sam 11:2–4), Uriah goes and lies on "his bed" with the servants of his Lord, but he did not go down to his house" (1 Sam 11:13). It is as if Uriah knew that his bed had already been desecrated by this powerful man, the king of Israel and Judah.

"In the morning," a time when a person ought to come to his senses, David writes the death sentence of Uriah. He asks Joab to forcibly put him and other valiant soldiers in severe harm's way so that he will die. In most English translations it is written as, "David wrote a letter to Joab" (KJV, NIV, NRSV). In Hebrew, the word which is translated as "letter" is *Sepher*. This is the word which is used for "The Book, *Sepher* of the Covenant" which the LORD gave to Moses, and which was read in the hearing of all the people (Exod 24:7). More significantly, according to the Torah, it was required that every king, before he becomes king, would "write for himself in a Book, (*Sepher*) a copy of this Torah approved by the Levitical priests" (Deut 17:18).

This is a crucial point. Instead of doing what the Torah required him to do, David was rewriting the Torah according to the models of the laws set by the kings of the ancient Near East. This would most definitely lead to gross injustice and evil, as was seen in the kingdoms of the other nations. David was the first king to rewrite the constitution of Israel. This was the pattern which was followed by later kings of Israel and Judah, and it led to a horrible state of society in Israel. It led to the constant repetition of the phrase regarding the kings of Israel and Judah, they "did evil in the eyes of the LORD." Solomon did evil (1 Kgs 11:6), Asa did evil (1 Kgs 15:26), and so on (1 Kgs 15:34; 16:7, 19, 25, 30; 22:18, 52; 2 Kgs 8:18, 27; 13:2, 11; 14:24; 15:9, 18, 24, 28; 17:2; 21:2, 9, 20; 23:32, 37; 24:9, 19). The rewriting of the Torah led to endemic and systemic evil in Israelite society.

SOLOMON AND THE #METOO MOVEMENT

Here I will briefly mention the case of Solomon. In the text where it says, "Solomon did evil," it specifies the nature of the evil. It is a multiplication of what happens when the kings rewrite the Torah. Solomon brought in 700 women who were temple priestesses/princesses in the surrounding nations, and 300 sexual slaves (1 Kgs 11:3). He worshipped Ashtoreth, the Sidonian goddess of sex and war. This goddess was the same as the Sumerian goddess Inanna (1 Kgs 11:5). In Jerusalem, he built a temple for the Moabite god Chemosh, where boys were sacrificed (1 Kgs 11:7).

Rehoboam, Solomon's son, multiplied the systems of evil initiated by his father. There is one poignant moment when the people of the Northern tribes came to Rehoboam and said, "Your father made our yoke heavy (*qasha*). Now please lighten the harsh enslavement (*avodah*) of your father, and his heavy (*qasha*) yoke on us, and we will serve you" (1 Kgs 12:4). Rehoboam asked the people of the North to return after three days, to hear his judgment. When they returned, "he answered the people harshly (*qasha*) . . . saying, 'My father made your yoke heavy. I will add to your yoke. My father disciplined you with whips, but I will discipline you with scorpions'" (1 Kgs 12:13, 14).

It should be noted that these same categories of injustice and servitude were used to describe the harsh enslavement and injustices which the King of Egypt promulgated against his Hebrew slaves: "He made their lives bitter with harsh service" (*avodah qasha*, Exodus 1:14).

The narrative of David and Solomon and the rest of the kings shows that Judah and Israel had become like the old Egypt. David and his descendants did to their own people what the cruel Egyptians did to their forefathers.

Miriam, the sister of Moses, and the women led a #MeToo movement then. Sadly, it does not seem like there was a #MeToo movement during the reign of Solomon.

Thankfully, there was a #MeToo movement during the time of his son Rehoboam. It resulted in the division of the country into ten tribes which formed the Northern Kingdom of Israel, and two tribes which formed the Southern Kingdom of Judah.

DID URIAH DIE WILLINGLY?

Uriah's answer to the king made it clear to him that he was ready to die. He said:

> "The ark and Israel and Judah are staying in tents, and my commander Joab and my lord's men are camped in the open country (*'al pene ha sadeh*, literally, upon the face of the field). How could I go to my house to eat and drink and make love to my wife? As surely as you live, I will not do such a thing!" (2 Sam 11:11 NIV)

The Hebrew phrase *'al pene ha sadeh* is always used of someone or an animal being sacrificed (Lev 17:5; Num 19:16; Ezek 29:5). The king instructed Joab in the *sepher* to "place Uriah in the forefront of the hardest fight, and then draw back from him, that he may be struck down and die." (2 Sam 11:14). According to the narrative, Uriah dies with the *Anshe Chayil*, the spiritually, physically, mentally, and emotionally strong men. This was the same word used to describe Ruth in the previous section, and the valiant woman, *Eshet Chayil*, of Proverbs 31. What a life. David thought he had finished Uriah off, but the text makes it clear that Uriah knew he was going to die. Did Uriah die willingly? The Hebrew words of this narrative make it clear that he knew that King David had desecrated his wife. What was there to live for now? He died a horrible, yet honorable death.

The text says, "When the wife of Uriah heard that her husband was dead, she wailed" (*saphad*; 2 Sam 11:26). This is a loud, public form of lament and mourning. It is heartfelt and genuine. She lamented for the injustice which had been done to her husband. As soon as the seven-day period of mourning was over, David sent for her, and gathered her, alongside all the other women he had gathered. She became one of the women in his harem, women who were his sexual slaves. It may be noted that most English translations say, "David had brought her to his house, and she became his wife, and bore him a son" (2 Sam 11:27 NIV, NRSV, ESV). This misses the gravity of what David did, and what he presumably did to other women. The question that remains unanswered is, why would he be able to see a woman going through her cleansing rites, unless this was his practice, which he had borrowed from the divine kings of the other nations?

Movies have been made about Bathsheba, which portray her to be a seductress. This couldn't be farther from the truth. She was an honorable wife of an honorable man. Both were gentiles. Both were minorities. Both were poor aliens. Sadly, the most powerful man took her in as a sexual slave, just because that is what religions of that time gave him the power to do.

The prophetic conclusion is poignant, "But, this word, or philosophy of life, was evil, in the eyes of the LORD" (2 Sam 11:27). It seems to me that most English translations again water down the gravity of the Hebrew text by translating it as "The thing that David had done *displeased* the LORD (italics mine)" (NIV, NRSV, ESV). This did not merely displease the Lord. This was utterly evil.

The words and actions of Uriah, and his wife, Bathsheba, serve as amazing examples of the biblical #MeToo movement. These contrast with the actions of King David. The New Testament, in the Matthew 1 genealogy, stresses this by emphasizing that Bathsheba, for all time, will be known as the wife of Uriah.

NATHAN'S PARABLE: THE SHEEP AND THE SHEPHERD

The next chapter gives God's response to David's evil:

> The LORD sent Nathan to David. When he came to him, he said, "There were two men in a certain town, one rich and the other poor. The rich man had a very large number of sheep and cattle, but the poor man had nothing except one little ewe lamb he had

bought. He raised it, and it grew up with him and his children. It shared his food, drank from his cup and even slept in his arms. It was like a daughter to him. Now a traveler came to the rich man, but the rich man refrained from taking one of his own sheep or cattle to prepare a meal for the traveler who had come to him. Instead, he took the ewe lamb that belonged to the poor man and prepared it for the one who had come to him." David burned with anger against the man and said to Nathan, "As surely as the LORD lives, the man who did this must die! He must pay for that lamb four times over, because he did such a thing and had no pity." Then Nathan said to David, "You are the man!" (2 Sam 12:1–7 NIV)

The narrative seeks to make it clear that what follows is not merely Nathan's parable. Rather, this was the LORD's word to David, through Nathan. The Hebrew text gives the background of two men, one city, one poor, one rich. It creates a scenario where there is tension between two kinds of people, even though both are human, and both live in one city. Yet the fact that one should be classed as rich and one as poor is rather troubling. The Hebrew word for the rich man, *'Ashir,* is that of a person who has acquired wealth through unjust, sometimes violent means. (Mic 6:12; Prov 18:23; 22:7, 16; 28:6; Eccl 5:12). The Hebrew word for the poor man, *roosh,* is used of person who is poor because of systems of injustice which he has had to endure in life (Ps 82:3; Prov 13:23; 18:23; 19:7, 22; 29:13; Eccl 5:8). These are people who are born into this state of poverty. They have to face systems of injustice against them from the moment they are born into a *roosh* family (Eccl 4:14).

This introduction of the parable should have shocked David. If he and his society were really living by the Torah, there should not have been this kind of a distinction in society (Exod 22:21–25; 23:3; Lev 19:10; 23:22; Deut 15; 23:24–25, and so on). It is crucial that systems which lead to this kind of poverty, according to this story, be related to the treatment of Bathsheba at the hands of David. The rape of Bathsheba would not happen if the Hittites were not treated as third-rate citizens and low-class people.

In describing the difference between the rich man and the poor man, the narrative seeks to make clear that the former was very, very rich. The adjectives make him sound like a billionaire. He had many, many, many farm animals. In describing the poor man, the narrative says, "But the poor man had nothing, only one little ewe lamb." Notice the repetition of the word "one" in 2 Samuel 12:1 ("One rich, one poor") and 2 Samuel 12:3 ("one little ewe lamb"). This was a lamb that he had *qanah*, created. This is the same word which is used of Boaz's recreation of Ruth, and the economy around Ruth. This process of recreation is then described in this story in very intimate categories, "He gave her life; she grew up with him and his children; she shared his food, and drank from his cup; she lay on his bosom; she was a daughter to him," (2 Sam 12:3, my translation). These are powerful words. This ewe lamb was not merely a lamb. She was family.

The narrative goes on, "a traveler came to the rich man" (2 Sam 12:4). The word which is used to describe the traveler refers to a person of no consequence to the rich man, or perhaps everyone was a person of no consequence to him.

What he does next is more mindboggling. Most English translations say, "he refrained from (NIV)" or "he was unwilling to take one of his own flock" (2 Sam 12:4 ESV). The Hebrew word *Chamal*, literally means "he has pity, compassion on his own flocks." (It may be noted that later in the narrative, David himself comments that this man had no *chamal*, pity, 2 Sam 12:6) This was the reason he took the poor man's lamb, slaughtered her, and served her to this no-one traveler.

This sequence makes it clear that while human beings do have a sense of compassion, racial, economic, and social distinctions also make it possible for human beings to have compassion for one, and no compassion for the Other. This is what this rich man did.

David's response to this story is put in a rather dramatic form in the Hebrew. Literally "his short nostrils flared up, and flames burst out of them." The original readers of this narrative would not have missed the point that this would be the precise reaction of the divine kings of the ancient Near East. Canaanite mythology has fire coming out of the nostrils of Moloch, who consumes children. In Egyptian religion, the pharaoh wears the serpent on his head, which then spews fire. It seems like David is quite consumed by the image of being a king in the mould of the nations around him.

The God of the Bible, quite in contrast to this image of David, is described as "long suffering" (Exod 34:6; Num 14:18; Joel 2:13; Jonah 4:2; Nah 1:3; and so on). This phrase and description of God literally means, one "who has a long nose." That is why he is so gentle, compassionate, gracious, and abounds in faithfulness, etc. This is the complete opposite of the gods and divine kings of the nations around Israel. Therefore, David's reaction was contrary to the virtues of God.

The sentence which David gave to this person is also contrary to the Torah. Nowhere in the Torah is a death sentence prescribed in the case of the killing of an animal. Nathan neither goes into the details of the Torah, nor does he comment on David's demeanor; instead he simply says, "You are the man." You are the rich man, '*Ashir*, the one who has acquired wealth through unjust, and violent means. This gave you the power to do whatever you wanted to do with the people who are poor because of systems of evil in your kingdom, systems which cause them to get into inextricable states of poverty. This causes evil things to happen to them. Therefore, "the LORD says to him, 'Why did you despise the word of the LORD by doing what is evil in his eyes? You struck down Uriah the Hittite with the sword and took his wife to be your own. You killed him with the sword of the Ammonites." (2 Sam 12:9 NIV)

It becomes clear from this that systems of evil always begin with the undergirding of religion or philosophy. That was the problem with David. He despised the word of the Lord. The Hebrew word translated as "despised" expresses an attitude of scorn when one looks down on something or someone, like how Esau despised his birthright (Gen 25:34), or when Michal despised her husband David when he was dancing (2 Sam 6:16). David despised the Torah, the word of God, and God himself, so he began following the laws of the divine kings. This worldview no doubt influenced society, and there were several "one cities" in his kingdom, where these kinds of things were happening. Obviously, as the following verses say, this kind of complex pattern of injustice and evil always carries on into the following generations. Sadly, it does not stop with one generation, unless that generation makes a clean break with systems of injustice at very deep levels. Unfortunately, this did not happen with the kingdoms of Israel and Judah. They eventually were exiled into places where they experienced the same things which were begun by David.

Uriah the Hittite, his wife, Bathsheba, and the poor man of Nathan's parable are all a part of the #MeToo movement of the Bible. It is crucial to note that Nathan the prophet is also a part of the #MeToo movement. Prophets of the Bible always are a part of the #MeToo movement.

The prophetic evaluation of the life of David makes it clear that the biblical #MeToo movement sees it as a complex problem. Yes, it is a person in power, very similar to the Hollywood and media dons of our time who are the main perpetrators of sexual violence against women. This narrative underlines the problem of power. Had David realized that the only reason he had power was because of God's grace in his life; had he remained faithful to God, as he had been in his early days; had he written for himself a copy of the Torah; and had he read it every day of his kingly life; he might not have committed this evil (Deuteronomy 17:14-20) . This is the religious, sin dimension of the problem that the biblical #MeToo movement is raising. Kings of that day were given the religious sanction to engage in sexual violence against women, especially women in the lower classes of society, or foreign women. David, on the other hand, would have known better had he followed the Torah.

The narrative makes it clear that failure in the religious realm always lead to complex evils at the social, economic, and legal levels, and a whole lot more.

Nathan raises these complex issues in his parable, as he undergirds the #MeToo movement started by Uriah and Bathsheba.

The biblical #MeToo movement is a very complex movement.

6

The Marys in the Book of Genesis and the #MeToo Movement

The very first thing that a reader of the New Testament encounters when reading from the beginning of Matthew is the genealogy of Jesus the Messiah. It begins with the words, "The book of the generations of Jesus the Messiah." It is a book which is written to complete the narrative of the book of Genesis, which it highlights at crucial junctures, ten times, "These are the generations of . . ." (Gen 2:4; 6:9; 10:1; 11:10; 11:27; 25:12; 25:19; 36:1; 36:9; and 37:2). The book of Matthew, and the introduction to the whole New Testament, shows that Jesus the Messiah is setting right all the evils found in the generations of human history.

What are these evils? The New Testament answer is "Look at the lives of these five women highlighted in Matthew 1." Jesus the Messiah—the son of Abraham, the son of David, indeed the Son of God—has come to wipe out the evils which are found in the narratives of these five women. These five women are emblematic of all the evil that women have had to endure throughout the history of humanity, and the mission of Jesus the Messiah faces these issues head-on, for indeed, this was the main mission of Jesus the Messiah.

A LIFE OF BITTERNESS

We encountered a very poignant moment in the Ruth narrative when Naomi returned from Moab after ten long years of horrible life in exile.

The women of Bethlehem remembered her and were very excited to see her. They said, "This is Naomi." She responds, "Don't call me *Naomi*, the joyful one, call me *Mara*, the bitter one" (Ruth 1:20–21)! She said her life has been bitter.

The four women whose lives we have examined in this book have also seen bitterness in their lives. Bitterness, which is a result of contempt for the weak and the marginalized, and the resultant evil and injustice against women, in particular. The question before us is: why does the introduction to the gospel seek to highlight this theme? Is it that the gospel of Jesus the Messiah is told in the four Gospels to address all of these areas of the bitterness of the Marys of the Bible, and the Marys of the world?

The book of Matthew stresses that the gospel of Jesus the Messiah was essentially a #MeToo movement. In the previous chapters we have seen this through the lives of all the four Marys of the Bible. In this chapter I would like to show how the #MeToo movement of the book of Matthew really points to the generations found in the book of Genesis since it is in fact the original #MeToo movement. The Gospel of Matthew and the other Gospels are a culmination of the #MeToo movement in the Bible.

A

THE CREATION NARRATIVE AND THE #METOO MOVEMENT

God as Mother

The creation narrative begins with the description of God as a mother. Genesis 1:2 describes it this way. "The earth was without form and void, and darkness was over the face of the deep. And the Spirit of God was fluttering (*merachefet*) over the face of the waters" (Gen 1:2). The verb "fluttering" or "hovering" is a feminine verb. This is the picture which is given of a mother eagle who flutters over her little eaglet, whom she is seeking to teach to fly (Deut 32:11). In keeping with this thought, God is portrayed both as Father and Mother throughout the Torah. The same poem which describes God as a mother eagle, as if to reinforce this idea, also describes God as giving birth to Israel, "You have forsaken the Rock who bore you, you forgot the God who gave you birth" (Deut 32:18).

A good example of this is when Moses asked God to show him his glory. The following text reads,

> "And he said, 'I will make all my goodness pass before you and will proclaim before you my name "The LORD." And I will be gracious to whom I will be gracious, and will show mercy (*Racham*) on whom I will show mercy' (*Racham*) . . . The LORD passed before him and proclaimed, 'The LORD, the LORD, a God merciful (*Racham*) and gracious, slow to anger, and abounding in steadfast love and faithfulness.'" (Exod 33:19; 34:6)

The Hebrew word *Racham* literally means womb, as in God opening up Leah's and Rachel's wombs (Gen 29:31; 30:22). Therefore, the compassion and mercy of God come from his womb.

The prophet Isaiah describes God as a woman in labor and as a nursing mother on several occasions. In Isaiah 49:15, for example, the Lord exclaims, "Can a woman forget her nursing child, that she should have no compassion (*Racham*) on the son of her womb? Even these may forget, yet I will not forget you."

It seems to me that right from the very beginning, God is portrayed as a mother hovering over the birthing waters, ready to give birth to the universe. The waters are dark, but the light is ready to be birthed. All that God creates is good (*Tov*). There is essential goodness in all that God creates.

The creation narrative ends with the words, "These are the generations of the heavens and the earth when they were created" (Gen 2:4). It is as if "the heavens and the earth" are papa and mama. This process of co-creation sets the standard for how male and female identity issues are addressed in the book of Genesis.

Both the Man and the Woman are Created in the Image of God

Genesis 1:27 reads, "So God created mankind in his own image, in the image of God he created them; male and female he created them" (NIV). Here God has both male and female characteristics, which is a very crucial idea. It also sets the biblical idea of maleness and femaleness. Both form the biblical idea of God.

Both are given dignity. This is much in contrast to ancient Near Eastern societies, which considered women to be used and abused. The biblical creation narrative gives the woman equal dignity.

This is a crucial #MeToo statement.

The Two Shall be One

God is described as a complex person. There is a crucial Jewish creedal statement on the biblical idea of God. It comes from Deuteronomy 6:4, *Shma' Israel YHWH Elohenu, YHWH Echad*; Hear O Israel, YHWH is our God; YHWH is One (*Echad*)

In the creation narrative, regarding the place of man and woman in marriage, the text says, "Therefore shall a man leave his father and mother and cling to his woman, and the two shall become one (*Echad*)" (Gen 2:24).

I must underline a few things in this text. First, the word used to describe the oneness of the man and the woman is the same word which describes the Oneness of God. Somehow the man and the woman together as one are a description of God. Second, in most ancient Near Eastern societies, as is true of many societies today, it is the woman who leaves her father and mother and becomes a part of the harem of her husband, or she essentially gets married to the husband's family. This leads to much abuse of women. She is subject to the whims and fancies of not only her husband, but also the patriarch of the family. This text makes it clear that it is the man who leaves his parents' house and becomes one with the woman. And finally, it is the man who cleaves to the woman. Not the opposite. The woman is the more powerful person in the family. These crucial points are very important #MeToo factors in the creation narrative.

Human sexuality is therefore described as an experience of becoming one like God is One. This is a very high order of understanding human sexuality. It is not merely an act to pacify one's sexual urges or desires, but rather an experience in which one experiences oneness, just like God is One.

This experience of sexuality can only happen through mutual honor and faithfulness between a man and a woman. This faithfulness is described in the next verse, "The man and his wife were both naked (*arum*) and were not ashamed." The Hebrew word *arum* describes transparency between two individuals. This can only happen between a couple, when a man leaves everything to cleave to a woman. It cannot happen when a man seeks to fulfill his sexual urges at the expense of a woman, especially a woman he does not know or care about.

This is a strong #MeToo principle of the Bible.

Why Was the Woman Created? What are the Purposes of Being a Woman and the #MeToo Movement?

What About the Woman as the Helper?

Much has been made of the creation narrative, which describes the woman as only a helper or helpmate to man. It would be good to explore this allegation against the Bible.

The Genesis narrative of this section begins with the following words, as written in the following English translations of Genesis 2:18:

> And the Lord God said, "*It is* not good that the man should be alone; I will make him an help meet for him." (KJV)

> The LORD God said, "It is not good for the man to be alone. I will make a helper suitable for him." (NIV)

> Then the LORD God said, "It is not good that the man should be alone; I will make him a helper as his partner." (NRSV)

In each of these translations, it seems like the woman is given a very secondary role. She is created for man, to be a helper of sorts—KJV, "help meet for him"; NIV, "helper suitable for him"; and NRSV, "helper as his partner." These translations, for one thing, are not in conformity with the Genesis 1 text, where the two sexes are equal. The Hebrew words used to describe the woman are *Ezer Kenegdo*. A cursory survey of the first word, *Ezer*, will lead us to understand that this word always refers to God himself. In Exodus 18:4, it describes the name of one of Moses' sons, Eliezer, "my God, my help." In Deuteronomy 33, Moses, in his final song, describes the Lord as *Ezer* (Deut 33:7, 29); In several of the psalms, God is described as *Ezer*. Psalm 148:5 says, "Blessed are those whose *Ezer* is the God of Jacob" (see also Ps 146:5 NIV; 20:2; 70:5; 89:19; 121:1, 2; 124:8). The prophets constantly accuse the people of revolting against the Lord, their *Ezer* (Hos 13:9). It becomes clear that the word *Ezer* does not refer to an ordinary person. If the rest of the Bible refers to this person being God himself, what does it say about the place of the woman in society?

The second word, *kenegdo*, is an adverb. It means "one who goes before another person," as in Genesis 33:12, where Esau seeks to go ahead of Jacob and his family; or the angel of the Lord, who went ahead of the people (Josh 5:13). In light of this phrase, it seems like the woman is, as an *Ezer kanegdo*, given a very strong persona and a position of privilege. This, again, seems to be a very strong #MeToo message. Much of the violence and abuse of women, then and now, is because of the inferior position which is given to them. Because of this inferior position in society, men in positions of power have taken advantage of women.

This Hebrew phrase, *Ezer kanegdo*, which is used in the very first description of the woman in the Bible, is perhaps the most crucial #MeToo statement of the Bible. The fact that it occurs in the creation narrative sets the agenda of the entire Bible, especially in the context of ancient Near Eastern creation narratives. Here is a glimpse from Enuma Elish, the Babylonian creation story,

> Tiamat, the mother of all, gave birth to peerless and hideous monsters; Serpents with fangs for teeth, snakes with venom for blood;

> Terrifying dragons, filled with divine power; to see them was to die, once prepared to strike, they were invincible. (Enuma Elish, 1:132–38)

> Marduk rounded up the monsters of Tiamat; He brought them as trophies before the divine assembly . . . (Enuma Elish, V:71)

> I will knead blood and bone (of Tiamat) into a slave, "Aborigine" will be his name. Verily, slave man I will create. He shall be a slave to the gods. That they might be at ease. It was Kingu who contrived the uprising (against Marduk) and made Tiamat rebel. They bound him and held him before Ea. They imposed on him his guilt, and severed his blood vessels. Out of his blood they fashioned the human being. (Enuma Elish, VI:5–8; 30–40)

Human beings are created from the blood of the demoness, Tiamat, and her consort, Kingu. Human beings are despicable creatures, since they are associated with the demoness Tiamat.

Similar to creation narratives of this kind, the laws pertaining to women in writings like the Code of Hammurabi (ca 1790–1750 BCE) also place women in a very inferior place. Following are some laws from the code of Hammurabi.

- If a wife robs her husband when he is dead, she is to be put to death, the receiver of the property is to be put to death. (CH 19)

- If the husband is alive he may punish his wife as he likes. If the receiver is a slave, he/she loses both nose and ears and the husband may cut off his wife's ears. (CH 21)

- When a woman squanders her husband's possessions, she destroys his honor. She must die by drowning. (CH 144)

- A temple priestess/prostitute *ugbabtu* who enters a public space must be put to death by fire. (CH 110)

It seems clear the ancient Near Eastern religions and societies did not regard women as human. It encouraged high-class men to abuse women. Creation narratives, religious rituals, and laws were designed to abuse women. The biblical creation narrative was written in the context of these myths and laws, and is designed to counteract this awful perspective of women in society. This is the original #MeToo movement of the Bible.

B

GENESIS 3, THE NARRATIVE OF EVE AND THE FALL

Genesis 3 is usually regarded as the narrative of the fall of humanity. It is usually taught in Sunday school classes that man fell because the woman disobeyed God. She took from the forbidden fruit, and gave to her man, who ate it as well. So they fell, and ever since then, human beings have been fallen sinners.

It seems to me that this understanding of Genesis 3 is rather simplistic, and has given kids a very wrong impression of women. It is generally assumed by some that women are gullible and therefore they should not be trusted to make good judgments. After all, it was the woman who was enamored by the voice of a talking snake, and it led to the disobedience of the primeval parents. It is generally assumed, as a corollary to this, that women leaders will lead men astray if they are given leadership roles. So, in the eyes of some, women should not be given leadership positions. If Adam was a true leader, he would not have listened to the voice of Eve.

These simplistic understandings of Genesis 3 have, it seems to me, misled generations of young people. It would be more appropriate to interpret the Genesis 3 narrative in the light of its ancient Near Eastern context. The readers of Moses would be able to see this context clearly. Modern readers need to do a little more work to understand the context of the Genesis 3 narrative.

In Genesis 3:1 we encounter the snake, who is described as, "more crafty than any of the wild animals the LORD God had made." Both the

NIV and the NRSV describe the snake as "more crafty." The NLT describes the serpent as "the shrewdest of all the wild animals the LORD God had made." In all of these translations, the snake is described with negative characteristics, yet the Hebrew makes it clear that this is the same word which is used to describe the man and the woman, in the previous verse: "Adam and his wife were both naked, and they felt no shame" (Gen 2:25 NIV). The word that is translated as "naked" in Genesis 2:25, is the same word which is translated as "crafty" or "cunning" in Genesis 3:1. It is the word *arum*. In Genesis 2:25, the English translations portray it is a good, positive, and innocent characteristic. In Genesis 3:1, it is portrayed as a negative characteristic.

In the narrative, the serpent comes to the woman and says, "Really, God said you shall not eat from all the trees of the garden" (Gen 3:1)! This was more of a challenge than a question. Two questions arise out of this: First, what was the nature of the challenge? And second, was this really a talking animal? The answers to these two questions are found in a study of ancient Near Eastern religions. In Sumerian, Egyptian, and Syrian religions, there is ample evidence of the worship of the snake gods and goddesses throughout these regions.[23] There is also evidence that women were forced to be temple prostitutes to these gods under fig trees or grape vines in ancient Near Eastern religions.[24] These temple prostitutes were usually given a sacred drink which is intoxicating. The religious/ritual sexual encounter between a priest/man, and the temple prostitute (*Ugbabtu*, in Sumerian religions), it was thought, caused them to become divine.

This practice may also be seen in several world religions even today. Much research is done in the Devadasi System of India. Underage girls are married to gods and goddesses. They then have to live in temples. There under sacred trees, they have to participate in sexual rituals, with high-caste men, after they partake of the "sacred drink."[25]

In some parts of India, when a young woman of low-caste or outcast standing becomes of marriageable age, she must first live in the temple and have sexual encounters with the priest; only then may she be married to another young man from her caste. However, it is made clear to the young

---

23. See, e.g. Miller Bonney, "Disarming the Snake Goddess," 171–90.

24. Keel and Uehlinger, *Gods, Goddesses, and Images*; Mazar, "'Bull Site,'" 27–42; Ussishkin, "Ghassulian Shrine at En Gedi," 1–44; Mazar, "Sacred Tree," 31–37.

25. Shingal, "Devadasi System," 107–23.

bridegroom that she is really the bride of the god, or really the priest of the god. She is only loaned to him for a season of time.

Ancient Near Eastern religions give evidence of other animals also being used for the purposes of religious rites, which abuse girls. These include horses, eagles, cows, cats, jackals, swine, lions, cobras, frogs, dogs, bulls, etc. These animals were associated with the Egyptian pantheon of gods: *Horus, Neferrum, Ra, Sekhmet,* and the pharaoh.[26]

Genesis 3 shows that the worship of the serpent under the Tree of Knowledge was the most malicious form of worship. Serpents, in ancient Near Eastern religions, were also used to do harm to low-class human beings, especially women. The snake goddess, Renenutet, spat fire upon masses should they seek to revolt against the royalty. This goddess in Middle Egyptian religion became known as *Apep.* The entire world rested on the divine serpent. Egyptian pharaohs who were divine beings, and who came out of the river Nile, always wore a snake around their crowns. Often, the depiction of the snake is around the papyrus tree, from which emerges Egyptian knowledge of divinity.

It seems clear that the Genesis 3 narrative is a powerful #MeToo *apologia* against this kind of use of animals and plants, in the religions of the Sumerians and the Egyptians. Animals like snakes and cows, and plants like the sacred fig tree, were used to do evil against the large majority of the low-class people.

The myth of the snake and the tree is also found in the religions of South Asia. In Buddhism, Buddha sat under the Buddha tree, *Nyagrodha,* or peepal tree, and upon a snake, to achieve the state of Buddha, Knowledge. In Aryan Hinduism, the Rig Veda 1.164, tells the mythical story of the *Jiva* and the *Atman.* The *Jiva* (woman soul) partakes of the intoxicating fig tree, and then has a sexual encounter with the *Atman* (the divine man), which results in the deification of both the *Jiva* and the *Atman.* Sadly, it leads to more abuse and rape of women, in the South Asian context.

Nakedness

Nakedness is a crucial theme in much of world. In India, where I come from, women are never supposed to show any part of their body. This is true of all religions in India. All women, regardless of region or religion, are not supposed to show any part of their body. I remember watching movies

26. Ikram, *Divine Creatures.*

where the camera would focus on the feet of a woman, but that was the most that the camera was allowed to show. Unless, of course, the woman was a prostitute. In light of this, all rapes in India have been justified by the following sets of questions and statements.

Why was she out when it was getting dark?

Why was she not wearing traditional garments, like the *salwar-kameez* or the *saree*?

Why was she wearing jeans?

Why was she wearing a dress?

Why was she not wearing the head covering in public?

Why was she showing her face in public?

The list of questions and statements can go on and on. Similar questions and statements are made in much of the world, and the #MeToo movement has brought this to the attention of people across the world.

Nakedness and Shame

The Genesis narrative begins with the simple statement: "The man and his woman were both naked (*Arum*) and they were not ashamed" (Gen 2:25).

This word is repeated again in Genesis 3:7. This time the man and the woman "know that they are naked," but they are ashamed and use the leaves of the tree of the knowledge of good and evil, the fig tree, to sew garments for themselves.

The third time this word was used in this narrative is when they heard "the sound of the LORD walking in the spirit of the day. The man and the woman hid themselves from the presence of the LORD God" (Gen 3:8). The man responded to God's call with the words, "I heard your voice in the garden and I was afraid, because I was naked and I hid myself" (Gen 3:10). Nakedness was something of which they had not been ashamed, previously. However, now they were having two visceral responses: fear and and the urge to hide.

The ancient Near Eastern society, as is true of much of Eastern society today, is a society of honor and shame. There are things that one does which are considered honorable, and there are other things which are considered shameful. Honor and shame are always commensurate with the status of the individual in society. For example, a *dalit* woman in India had to go into a regular village with her breasts exposed, and a covering on her mouth. The exposure of her breasts was an indication of shame. The covering of her mouth, was also an indication of shame. Her very breath would desecrate the atmosphere—it would render the air unclean. A high-caste woman, on the other hand, would cover herself completely. One could only just see her face through the fluttering of the *sari*. This is also true in Middle Eastern society today. A woman of high standing would never expose any part of her body or face. It would be shameful if someone other than her husband saw her face. A woman of lower status might show her face, but that would be because she is a woman of lower status.

In Genesis 3, innocence gives way to shame, and this sadly puts women in a position where they end up being abused by males in society. God's response to this is crucial. He says, "Who told you about this kind of nakedness? Did you eat from the tree, which I commanded you not to eat, ritually eat" (Gen 3:11, my translation)? In ancient Near Eastern religions, the act of ritually eating from the intoxicating fruit of the fig tree always led to the rape of women, so this was forbidden in the Bible. Yet, this is what happens in Genesis 3.

Nakedness and human sexuality, which were supposed to be innocent and beautiful things, now have become the opposite. These are things which cause humanity to be afraid. When human beings are afraid, it causes others to do things which take advantage of that fear, awful things like rape. This is always done in secrecy.

That is why there needs to be a #MeToo movement to bring sexual crimes done in secrecy out into the open. Just like the fruit of the fig tree was used in ancient Near Eastern religions to abuse the bodies of women, so in today's society, powerful men use a modern-day "fruit of the tree" to intoxicate girls and rape them.

Craftiness and Nakedness

Genesis 2:25 declares that "the man and his woman were both naked (*Arum*) and were not ashamed." Genesis 3 is supposed to enter into a new chapter and a new topic, and so it is treated differently by the English-speaking world, and generally in the Bibles published in the West.

The chapter and verse divisions, it must be mentioned, were only introduced in the medieval era. Robert Estienne, a classical scholar and printer, is usually given credit for introducing chapter and verse divisions (1546–1551).

The original Hebrew text does not have chapter or verse divisions. Instead, there are liturgical reading sections, which are called *parashot*. They begin with an opening word, called *patuach*, and end with a closing word, called *sagoor*. In the case of Genesis 2 and 3, the *parasha* (i.e. the liturgical reading) begins with Genesis 2:4, and it ends with Genesis 3:15. The whole section holds together.

In light of this, it becomes doubly important to note that the *Arum*, the nakedness of the man and the woman, and its accompanying innocence are somehow related to the *Arum* of the serpent. The latter is translated as "the serpent was more crafty than any other beast of the field" (Gen 3:1), in all the English translations, and yet this same word is given a positive rendition in other parts of the Bible, as in this example: "Fools show their annoyance at once, but the prudent (*Arum*) overlook an insult" (Prov 12:16; see also 12:23; 13:16; 14:8, and so on). In some sense, therefore, the trait of the serpent should not be regarded as a negative trait; it is a wisdom trait. After all, if God created everything to be good (*tov*), then the serpent is also good. The problem lies in how human religions abuse the person and the image of the serpent, *nachash*.

In many ancient Near Eastern religions, the serpent was used to abuse girls and women from low classes of society. The worship of the *Nachash* was paramount in Egypt, especially the spitting cobra. Pharaoh was the firstborn god of the Egyptians, who descended from the sun god Re, and ascended from the divine river Nile. He always wore the *uraeus*, a spitting cobra, with a flared hood upon his forehead. The goddess Wadget was also depicted as a cobra-headed woman who spat fire on the enemies and the slaves of pharaoh. She was also the goddess of fertility. Egyptian pharaohs had sex with virgin girls to become more fertile and to reaffirm their divinity. This was also true of the Sumerian fertility god Ningizzida.

The early readers of the Torah quite clearly saw the import of this narrative in Genesis 3. It was an apologetic against *Nachash*, the serpent god, who was used by the Egyptian pharaohs to abuse and enslave other people groups, especially women, under specific tree centers of worship.

Exodus and the Serpent God

In the book of Exodus, the very first supernatural sign that Moses was given was the power over *Nachash*, the serpent god, who was responsible for the enslavement of his people. Notably, this sign was given to Moses at a particular tree: a bush. In Hebrew the word is *Seneh,* which is related to Mount *Sinai.* This was probably the Egyptian center for the worship of the serpent deity. For this reason, the Lord revealed himself to Moses at a "tree bush." The message the Lord was sending Moses is that the "tree bush," does not belong to *Nachash,* but rather to the Lord. In Deuteronomy 33:16, the Lord is described as one who dwells in *Seneh,* the bush.

We may also note that instead of *Nachash,* the fiery serpent god, in the Exodus 3 narrative, "the angel of the LORD appeared to him in a flame of fire (*labbah `Esh*)" (Exod 3:2).

Unfortunately, the same freed slaves, whose women were raped by the pharaohs in this snake ritual, then made an image of the bronze snake for themselves in the wilderness (Num 21:4–9). This image of the *Nachash* became the central focus of the abuse of girls, women, and orphans in the Jewish temple (2 Kgs 18:4).

Throughout history, sadly, the same motifs which are used to abuse women in a dominant culture are then used by the people of the same race or culture to abuse their own women. The prophets of the Bible then become the #MeToo prophets who preach against this kind of abuse of women.

The Gospel in Genesis 3

Genesis 3 reaches a crescendo in a piece of poetry found at the end of this narrative. It is God speaking to the serpentine religions, and it goes like this:

> The LORD God said to the serpent, Nachash
> Indeed you have done this
> You are lower than all the creatures
> And all the beasts of the field
> On your belly you shall walk
> Dust you shall eat
> All the days of your life
> I will put enmity between you and the woman
> Between your seed, and her seed
> He will bruise your head
> And You will bruise his heel. (Gen 3:14–15)

In the religion of the *Nachash,* the serpent was used as motif to abuse women. However, in this poem, God essentially says, "The woman will be equally powerful, and will stand up for her rights. She will humiliate the religion of *Nachash*, the serpent." This is a very powerful feminist text.

Taking things further, God says, "In human history, someone will emerge, called the seed of the woman. This seed of the woman will battle the seed of the serpent, the religion of *Nachash*, and will kill it. The religion of *Nachash* will certainly bruise the seed of the woman; however, the seed of the woman will eventually prevail."

There is a set of ancient Jewish translations called the Targums, which give a good understanding of this messianic poem. They posit that there are two kinds of religions and societies: those who follow the religion of the seed of the serpent, and those who follow the religion of the seed of the woman. Those who follow the religion of the seed of the serpent will always try to abuse the woman and the seed of the woman, the people of the Torah. This happens when the people of the Torah fail to adhere to the Torah. However, when those who are of the seed of the woman keep the Torah, they will bruise the religion of the *Nachash*, the seed of the serpent. This will continue to happen until the coming of the seed of the woman, par excellence, this is the Messiah. He will finally trample the religion of the *Nachash*, and the seed of the serpent.

The New Testament portrays Jesus to be this Messiah. The purpose of this Messiah is to save women, and the seed of the woman. He is bruised by the *Nachash* on the cross. However, he then overcomes death to defeat the religion of the *Nachash*.

Jesus' incarnation and death on the cross, from a rabbinic perspective, is a #MeToo movement. In the book of Matthew, it begins with the high-lighting of the five women. It ends with Jesus on the cross, being lifted up, just like the Egyptians lift up the serpent. At the cross, all the Marys of society witness him being bruised by the serpent. Nevertheless, he overcomes death and rises from the dead. The first witnesses to this event are also the Marys of the world. This is a profound #MeToo gospel.

Who is a Woman?

Right after this crucial Messiah #MeToo text, the narrative goes on to read, "The man called the name of his woman Eve (*Chavah*) because she was the mother of all life" (Gen 3:20). This is a very powerful sentence. The name of a person in the Bible, and in other ancient Near Eastern literature, is the identity of that person. A good example of this is in the narrative where

Moses encounters God at the burning bush, and God asks him to go to his enslaved people. Moses says, "If they ask me, 'What is his Name?' what shall I say to them?" God says to Moses "I AM who I AM" (Exod 3:13, 14). This was the identity of God. Everything flowed from him, because He is. Similarly, here in this text, the man recognizes that this person is, in essence the mother of all life. In many senses she is given divine status.

In the previous scene, the religions of the world, especially the religion of the *Nachash*, treated the woman as sexual property. Much in contrast to that, here the man recognizes that the woman is special. She is the mother of all life. This expression is a crucial corrective to much abuse of women in global society. Women are not merely sexual objects; they are people through whom life flows. This is truly powerful.

What is the Meaning of Sex?

The next scene in this narrative further reinforces the above idea. It reads, "The man knew (*yada'*) his woman (*Chavah*), and she conceived and bore Cain (*Qayin*). She exclaimed, 'I have created a man (*Qanah*)—the LORD'" (Gen 4:1).

This crucial text gives some very crucial building blocks to the #MeToo movement. The first, and in my estimation the most crucial one, is found in the first verb. What happened between Adam and Eve? It seems to me that some popular English translations miss the whole point. The New International Version says, "Adam made love to his wife Eve." The New Living Translation reads, "Now Adam had sexual relations with his wife." The New English Translation Bible reads, "Now man had marital relations with his wife." The Hebrew word is a very powerful one. It does not merely mean having sexual relations. The Hebrew word is *yada'*, which means having a deep, intimate, mental, emotional, psychological, social, and yes, physical knowledge of the other person.

This is the word which described the Tree of Knowledge in the previous chapters. In Exodus 3, when God reveals himself to Moses in the burning bush, he says to him, "I *know* their sufferings" (italics mine). Sadly, here again the NIV misses the gravity of the knowledge of God of the sufferings of the people by translating it as, "I am concerned about their suffering" (Exod 3:7). The Torah constantly urges the people to "know" the LORD. That is why he gave them the Torah (Deut 4:35, 39; 7:1; 9:3; and so on). In the Prophets, they always mourn the fact the people do not really "know" the LORD. Isaiah the prophet, for example, in his opening statement writes, "The ox *knows* its owner, and the donkey its master's crib, but Israel does not *know*, my people do not understand" (Isa 1:3, italics mine). The prophet Isaiah refers to the Suffering Messiah with the words, "He was despised and rejected by men, a man of sorrows, and one who *knew* grief" (Isa 53:3, italics mine). In a power passage regarding the new covenant, the prophet Jeremiah says, "I will put my Torah within them. I will write it on their hearts. And I will be their God, and they shall be my people. And no longer shall each one teach his neighbor, and each his brother, saying, '*Know* the LORD,' because they shall all *know* me" (Jer 31:33–34, italics mine).

It becomes clear from this very cursory survey of the Hebrew word *yada'* that the Hebrew understanding of an encounter between a man and a woman is a very deep, intrinsic knowledge. It is first mental, emotional, and spiritual. Only after one goes through these intrinsic facets of knowledge, may one engage in physical and sexual knowledge. If an encounter between a woman and a man is merely a physical encounter, it is wholly inadequate. At best it is 10 percent of the Hebrew word *yada'*.

If only human beings could understand the biblical understanding of an encounter between two human beings, there would be no sexual, emotional, and physical abuse.

The biblical word for sexual knowledge between two human beings is the same word which is used of human knowledge of God, and God's knowledge of human beings. If human beings understood and imbibed this, there would be no sexual and emotional abuse of women.

Woman as Creator

What did the woman do when she bore Cain? Here is how some of the English translations of Genesis 4:1 read. The venerable King James Version reads, "I have gotten a man from the LORD." The New Revised Standard Version reads, "I have produced a man with the help of the LORD." The New International Version reads, "With the help of the LORD, I have brought forth a man."

The word which is mostly translated as "gotten," (KJV), "produced, (NRSV), or "brought forth," (NIV), is a very important biblical #MeToo term. In Hebrew, the word is *qanah*. Sadly, in several English translations, this word is also translated as "buying" or "acquiring" the conquered people (i.e., Exod 21:2; Lev 22:11; Lev 25:45). It seems like the NIV translation of Genesis 14:19 has this word right. Melchizedek comes to Abraham, the great patriarch of the Old Testament, and gives him the following blessing, "Blessed be Abram by God Most High, Creator of heaven and earth" (Gen 14:19 NIV). The word which is translated as "Creator," is the much-maligned Hebrew word "*qanah!*" This incipient text defines the God of the Old Testament with the same Hebrew word, *Qanah*. This God is not a violent possessor and acquirer of captured slaves. He is a constructive Creator God.

In Genesis 4:1, going by this crucial and predominant usage of the term *qanah*, it would be more appropriate to translate the phrase as "I have created a man." This is a profound image of the woman. She is not just the bearer of a child, but rather a co-creator with God.

Boaz the Creator

In the chapter on Ruth, we have mentioned another poignant text where this much-maligned word is used. In the story of Ruth, a woman named Naomi goes and lives as a refugee in the land of Moab with her husband and sons because there is a famine in her own land. The men of the family die during this refugee sojourn in Moab. Naomi returns to her own land, Bethlehem, with her daughter-in-law Ruth, when she learns that the famine is over. The rest of the story of Ruth is a beautiful story. It is the story of two Hebrew words: *Goël* and *qanah*. Boaz and Ruth fall in love with each other, but he cannot marry her because there is another person, a *Goël* or kinsman redeemer, who is supposed to marry her. This person is supposed to first redeem the property for Naomi and Ruth, and then he is supposed to marry Ruth.

Here is how most English Bible translations put the dialogue that happens in Ruth chapter 4. Boaz says to this other kinsman redeemer,

> "Naomi, who has come back from the country of Moab, is selling the parcel of land that belonged to our kinsman Elimelech. So I thought I would tell you of it, and say: Buy it in the presence of those sitting here, and in the presence of the elders of my people. If you will redeem it, redeem it; but if you will not, tell me, so that I may know; for there is no one prior to you to redeem it, and I come after you." So he said, "I will redeem it." Then Boaz said, "The day you *acquire* the field from the hand of Naomi, you are also *acquiring* Ruth the Moabite, the widow of the dead man, to maintain the dead man's name on his inheritance." At this, the

next-of-kin said, "I cannot redeem it for myself without damaging my own inheritance. Take my right of redemption yourself, for I cannot redeem it." (Ruth 4:3–6 NRSV, italics mine)

On the surface, all seems well and good, except that after a closer look, Ruth and the property are both treated on the same level: as properties to be bought and sold. This is horrible. A closer look at the Hebrew word will reveal that this is the same word as the one that is used in Genesis 14:19. Boaz is not asking the kinsman redeemer to "acquire" or "buy" either the land or Ruth. Boaz is asking for a "recreation" of a new agrarian economy and society, and the recreation of a new woman, who has been destroyed by Moabite society. The society around them had destroyed economics, which led to poverty and slavery, and the society around them had also led to the sanctioned abuse of women, especially foreign women like Ruth. Boaz basically says, "We need the recreation of economics and women's identity." The other so-called kinsman redeemer is not willing to do this, so Boaz says, "I will do this." In Genesis 14:19, God is described as the "Creator (*qanah*) of heaven and earth." Ruth 4:4–10 uses the same word, *qanah*, five times to describe what Boaz does to the land and Ruth. He recreates a new economy and a new woman. God expects human beings to do the same in modern society. He disdains the acquiring of slaves and the promotion of abusive economic systems. The mission of the people of God is recreation, because God is a recreator.

The woman in Genesis 4:1 is called a creator. Sadly, in human history, women have been destroyed by men. However, men like Boaz are called upon to recreate women, as they were created in the Genesis creation narrative to be co-creators with God.

Both of these scenarios are very powerful.

Who Did the Woman Bear?

Most English translations provide some extra words to make the text flow better, so the venerable King James Version reads, "I have gotten a man from the LORD." The New Revised Standard Version reads, "I have produced a man with the help of the LORD." The New International Version reads, "With the help of the LORD, I have brought forth a man." It should be noted that the Hebrew does not have the words "with the help of." Those are provided in the English to make the translation smoother. However, in the process, the reader of the English translation loses the #MeToo significance of the text. Literally, the text should read as follows: "I have created a man—the LORD."

This follows directly from the poem in Genesis 3:15, the "seed of the woman" text. Genesis 4:1 is an interpretation of this Messiah text. The woman is not just described as the creator. She is also described as the bearer of God.

From a Hebrew literary perspective, this does not happen till much later in history, when Mary, the mother of Jesus, becomes the bearer of the LORD. She is the ultimate referent of the seed of the woman prophecy of Genesis 3:15, and of Genesis 4:1. The angel of the LORD comes to Mary in Matthew 1:23, and quotes another Messiah text, Isaiah 7:17, "The virgin will conceive and give birth to a son, and they will call him Immanuel (which means, "God with us.")."

Genesis 4:1, Isaiah 7:17, and Matthew 1:23 all are very strong #MeToo intertexts. Eve and Mary are both elevated to the status of the God-bearer.

C

THE DAUGHTERS OF MEN IN NOAH'S FLOOD,
AND THE #METOO MOVEMENT

The narrative of Noah's flood is an intriguing one. There are over twenty-five movies based on the flood. These include a 1928 and 1959 movie called *Noah's Ark*; a 1966 classic, *The Bible: In the Beginning*, directed by John Huston; a movie called *Many Waters*, based on a 1986 novel by Madeleine L'Engle; a 2014 movie called *Noah*; and so on. There are also TV series based on the flood, like *Superbook: Noah and the Ark* (2013) and *Siyaya: Come Wild with Us: Noah's Ark* (2014).

In these movies, God is generally portrayed as an angry God, rather like a spoiled angry being who just decided to commit genocide. What these writers and movie producers fail to realize is the biblical narrative provides the reader with background information to Noah's flood. It is found in Genesis 6:1–8, the prologue to the flood narrative.

> When human beings began to increase in number on the earth and daughters were born to them, the sons of God saw that the daughters of humans were beautiful, and they married any of them they chose. Then the LORD said, "My Spirit will not contend with humans forever, for they are mortal; their days will be a hundred and twenty years." The Nephilim were on the earth in those days— and also afterward—when the sons of God went to the daughters of humans and had children by them. They were the heroes of old, men of renown. The LORD saw how great the wickedness of the human race had become on the earth, and that every inclination of the thoughts of the human heart was only evil all the time. The

LORD regretted that he had made human beings on the earth, and his heart was deeply troubled. (Gen 6:1–6 NIV)

In ancient Jewish commentaries there is much discussion around the question of the nature of society during the days of Noah, the nature of the sin, and questions like, "Who are these sons of God? And who are these daughters of humans?" Midrash Rabbah, for example, posits that this was gross sexual immorality (Gen Rab 70:12).

An ancient Jewish commentary on this section of Genesis is found in the book of Enoch. It was probably written around 300 BC. The whole text of the book of Enoch is found in an ancient Ethiopian language called *Ge'ez*. There are also sections of the book of Enoch in a language called Aramaic, a language commonly spoken for about 200 years before the time of Jesus, and during the time of Jesus. This is essentially a narrative commentary on the first few chapters of Genesis.

The following is an excerpt from fragments of the book of Enoch found in Cave 4 of the Dead Sea Scrolls:

> The divine leaders forcibly took for themselves women for all, and they began to go into them and to defile them, and began to show them sorcery, and sexual spells. And they became pregnant through these rituals, and bore divine giants, three thousand cubits high, who were born according to their birth . . . The divine giants conspired to slay men and to devour them. They also began to practice sexual sin against all birds and beasts of the earth, and reptiles, and the fish of the sea, and began to devour the each other's flesh, and drink each other's blood. (4QEnoch, 4Q201, col III, my translation[27])

In this text, the sons of God are regarded as supernaturally endowed human beings, i.e. human beings who are possessed by fallen angels. These sons of God would take common women, give them ritual drinks, and forcibly have sex with them. The progeny who were born as a result of this ritual sex were called Nephilim (literally, "the fallen gods"). These gods were worshipped by humanity.

Rashi is a crucial medieval rabbi (AD 1040–1105). In his commentaries he makes much use of ancient rabbis, and texts like the book of Enoch. In his commentary on Genesis 6, Rashi uses the Rabbinic Midrash, Genesis Rabbah 26:5, "The generation of the Flood was not blotted out of the world

---

27. For another good translation see Martinez and Watson, *Dead Sea Scrolls Translated*, 247.

until they had written nuptials between males and between man and beast
... wherever you find lewdness and idolatry, punishment of an indiscriminate character comes upon the world killing good and bad alike."[28] Rashi goes on to comment that when Genesis 6:12 refers to "all flesh had corrupted its ways," it refers to the use of animals also in these bizarre sexual orgies. As a result of this, both human beings and animals are infected with disease.

It seems clear from the material I have researched that the prologue to Noah's flood is dealing with essentially an ancient #MeToo moment. Religion was used by men in high places who called themselves sons of God. They performed bizarre sexual rites on common women. They also used a variety of animals in these bizarre rituals. The result of this was Noah's flood.

It seems clear to me, that God heard the #MeToo cries of the daughters of women, the common women. It seems like, again, the English translations miss the attitude of God toward the horrible abuse of girls, women, and animals. The New Internation Version says, "the LORD regretted that he had made human beings on the earth." (Genesis 6:5; see also NRSV, ESV), and the New Living Translation says, "He was sorry." The Hebrew word is very telling of the demeanor of God concerning this horror. It is the word *nacham*. Just a few lines before this, this word is related to the name of the main character, Noah, which in Hebrew is *Nuach*. His name is called Noach, because "he will bring comfort (*nacham*) from our work and from our painful servitude" (Gen 5:29). This was the mission of Noah, right in the midst of all the pain and suffering women were experiencing. It is as if he and God heard the cries of the #MeToo women.

Noah's flood was a response to the cries of the #MeToo "daughters of men." It was to bring *nacham*, comfort to them (Gen 6:6). Restlessness, violence, sexual immorality, and sexual deviance were the core issues during the time of Noah which led to unimaginably horrible experiences for the daughters of man, at the hands of the greedy sons of God. This complex set of appalling events is at the core of sexual abuse, even today in global society. I have seen it in Africa and Asia. God's response to this dreadful string of happenings is *nacham* and *Nuach*—compassion and restfulness. These are deep responses, and not merely superficial and angry ones. *Nacham* is always God's response to human evil and violence (Judg 2:18). It is what God expects of his people, people like Boaz, who encounters Ruth—a

28. Neusner, *Genesis Rabbah*, 282–83.

trafficked woman (Ruth 2:13). In the context of violence and abuse, Psalm 23 expresses the hope that, "Even though I walk through the valley of the shadow of death. I fear no evil; for you are with me. Your rod and your staff, they comfort (*Nacham*) me." (Ps 23:4; also Ps 86:17; 90:13). In the context of much abuse, during the exile, which is the neo-Egypt enslavement experience, God always cries out, "*Nachamu Nachamu Ami*! Comfort, Comfort my people!" (Isa 40:1).

Noah's flood is a restful (*Nuach*), compassionate (*Nachamu*), and comforting response to the cries of the daughters of man. It requires a deep cleansing, one that can only come from the water. Water, throughout the Bible, is a source of deep cleansing. It is a symbol of creation and recreation. Genesis 1:2, for example, says, "The Spirit of God was hovering over the face of the waters" to bring about creation. In Exodus 14–15, the enslaved community of Israel "passed through the waters" of the Red Sea (Exod 14:21–22), to be cleansed and recreated. Before they entered the promised land, the new community of freed people went through the waters of the River Jordan (Josh 3:14–17). This was so they could enter into the promised land as a cleansed community, to bring about a deep change in the society among whom they were going to live. Their mission was to rescue abused women like Rahab (Josh 2, 6). The Gospel of Matthew seeks to parallel these events in the life of Christ. Jesus goes into the wilderness for forty days, and then he gets baptized in the river Jordan (Matt 3). He did this to underline his mission to "bring about justice," usually translated as "fulfill all righteousness" (Matt 3:13). It seems clear to me that his mission was to bring about justice to abused women like Tamar, Rahab, Ruth, the wife of Uriah, and all the Marys of the Bible, so he went through the waters of the River Jordan. Noah's flood happened because God heard the #MeToo cries of the daughters of common humanity. The solution was a deep cleansing through the waters of the flood.

I teach in a PhD program in India, and so travel there twice a year. I was reared in a New Delhi slum. I saw women and girls in India suffer much abuse. In January 2013, I traveled to India to teach a group of students that was primarily made up of female students. When I was teaching, India was reeling from a horrible rape that happened on December 12, 2012. A low-caste young woman, a physiotherapy college student, was tortured and brutally gang raped by six men on a public transportation bus. Her boyfriend was also brutally beaten and thrown out of the bus. It was 9 p.m., they had just watched a movie together, and she was returning to her poor, low-caste parents. They knew that they could never get married, because he was high-caste and she was low-caste. For this reason, the whole society looked on her with disdain. The six men who brutally raped her were also low-caste. This is the irony of the abuse of women. They disdained her because she was with a high-caste young man. After brutally raping her on the bus all night, they threw her out of the bus. Eleven days after the horrible rape, she was flown to Singapore in an attempt to save her life. But the most advanced medical procedures were not able to save her. She died in surgery. Her injuries were too gruesome.

Women's groups and students in Delhi and across India took to the streets for several days and months. The Prime Minister of India at that time, Mr. Manmohan Singh, said that there needs to be a fundamental change in the moral fiber of India.[29]

Sadly, when I go to India and open the newspapers, I still read the same kind of stories—many, many, many women and girls are sexually abused daily. What is the answer? The answer of Noah's flood narrative is that the "fundamental change in the moral fiber" can only come about "through the cleansing of the waters."

29. "Delhi Gang-Rape Case," *Times of India*, December 29, 2012.

D

THE CRIES OF THE WOMEN OF SODOM AND GOMORRAH AND THE #METOO MOVEMENT

Throughout the book of Genesis, similar to the last section, God always hears the cries of the #MeToo women, girls, and boys. Genesis 18–19 focuses on the story of Sodom and Gomorrah. This is another narrative that is much misunderstood in modern literature.

The narrative begins with the appearance of "YHWH, the LORD" to Abraham at the Oaks of Mamre. However, when he looks up, he sees three men. The obvious question is, Who appears to Abraham: YHWH, the LORD, or three men? The answer in the narrative seems to be both. In Christian interpretation, this is the appearance of the preincarnate Messiah.

Why did the preincarnate Messiah appear to Abraham? This form of the revelation of God happened in very crucial times. The narrative gives us information about this:

> "The LORD said, 'Shall I hide from Abraham what I am about to do?' . . . The LORD said, 'Because the *cries* of Sodom and Gomorrah are great, and their sin is very grave. I will go down and see whether they have done altogether according to the *cries* that have come up to me." (Gen 18:17, 20, 21; italics mine)

The words that are translated as "cries" in this text are very crucial. In many senses, these are #MeToo cries.

The first word, which is used in Genesis 18:20, in Hebrew, is the word *za'aq*. This word is used to describe the very painful cries of slaves who are beaten mercilessly by the enslavers, as in Exodus 2:23. In the rest of the Bible, this is always how this word is used (Judg 3:9, 15; 6:6; Isa 65:19, and so on). It is the cry of slaves in deep distress and hopelessness.

The second word, which is used in Genesis 18:21, is a similar sounding word. In Hebrew, it is the word, *tsaʾaq*. They sound similar, yet there is a fine distinction. This is the cry of the martyrs, whose blood is spilt as a result of injustice and violence, as in Genesis 4:10 where the blood of Abel cries from the ground when he is murdered by his brother. They are the cries of a brother who cries out for justice, as in Esau's cry (Gen 27:34). It is the cry of people who are starving because of famines. These are the cries of people who are enslaved and brutally abused, as in the case of the slaves in Egypt (Exod 3:7). These are the cries that the LORD hears.

This second word is used, more importantly, of the cries of a woman, who is sexually and physically abused (Deut 22:27). Sadly, most cries throughout history are because of violence between brothers or cousins. It is women and girls who bear the brunt of this violence. Sexual abuse also happens at the hands of neighbors, bosses, colleagues, and the like. The most brutal form of sexual abuse suffered by women is sexual abuse as a method of war, as I have seen in Africa and South Asia.

God hears both kinds of cries of women—*zaʾaq* and *tsaʾaq*. He says, "I have surely seen the affliction of my women; I have heard their cry because of their abusers. I know their sufferings." (Exod 3:7, 9). That is why the LORD came down to Sodom and Gomorrah. That is why he always comes down into history. He sees, hears, and knows the cries of abused women.

E

THE BLACK EGYPTIAN SLAVE-GIRL, HAGAR, AND THE #METOO MOVEMENT

In the Abrahamic narratives of the book of Genesis, God promises Abraham that he will provide a "seed (*zera'*)." This begins when Abraham is seventy-five years old, when he first leaves Ur in Mesopotamia and enters the promised land, in obedience to God's call. In Genesis 12:7, God says, "To your seed I will give this land." This promise is repeated often for a number of years, in subsequent texts (Gen 13:15, 16). Abraham keeps complaining to God. He says, "You keep promising. But, I have no seed." (Gen 15:3, my paraphrase). In response, God keeps reiterating his promise (Gen 15:5, 13, 18; 17:7, 8, 9; and so on).

In Genesis 16, Sarah gets tired of constantly hearing God's promises. So she decides to come up with a solution. Her solution is a black slave girl. Her name is Hagar. The Hebrew word for "slave girl" is *shiphchah*. It was a common practice for divine kings like the pharaohs and the equally divine royal officials to have a harem full of *shiphchahs*. These women were treated like physical properties of their owners. They did whatever they pleased with these women. This practice was not unlike the practice of slavery and the treatment of black slave women in the antebellum South, in the United States of America. Sexual abuse in harems is practiced even today in many parts of the world.

It is rather sad that the "man and woman of faith (Heb 11: 8, 11)" Abraham and Sarah, engaged in this awful practice. "Sarai said to Abram, 'You see that the LORD has prevented me from bearing children; go in to my slave-girl; it may be that I shall obtain children by her.' And Abram listened to the voice of Sarai." (Gen 16:2 NRSV)

Do most abuses of women happen with religion as an excuse? This text reveals that Sarah definitely blamed God for her condition, and thus it gave her the excuse to abuse another woman—a black slave woman. Unfortunately, it is not uncommon, historically, for women to take advantage of racially and socially lower-class women. One would think that Sarah would have known the dangers of being in this situation, being a woman herself. Further, her husband put her in positions where she could well have been abused by men in power. In those situations, Abraham thought his life was in danger, and so to save his own life, he used Sarah as a sexual pawn (Gen 12:10–20; and later Genesis 20). God protected Sarah, miraculously, in both of those dangerous and awful situations. Yet now this same Sarah turns around and puts her black female slave in a similar situation. She says, "Go into the slave-girl. She is our property. You can do whatever you want with her" (Gen 16:2, my translation). The imperative verb to "go into," is a very strong abusive term. She knew that this was the rape of a woman.

Another aspect of this sad narrative is that she was making full use of the laws of ancient Near Eastern society. Since Hagar was a slave girl and belonged to Abraham and Sarah, she was their property, and therefore, her children also belonged to them, especially the ones who were born of sexual intercourse between her and her master.

This practice was very common in the antebellum South. The children of slaves, especially those born as a result of the rape of slave-girls, belonged to the slave owners. This is true today in countries where bonded labor and debt slavery are practiced. I have seen this practiced in the villages of India, where whole families are owned by high-caste money lenders. The low-caste and outcast people get entrapped in intergenerational debt, also called bonded labor slavery. This usually happens because of one unfortunate health situation or calamity. This debt can never be paid off. It carries from one generation to the next. When a girl in the bonded labor family, gets her first menstrual cycle, she is taken away by the high-caste man, to serve as his sexual slave. This practice is very common in African countries as well. Recently, with a team, I spent some time in the largest refugee camp in the world, the Kakuma Refugee Camp, in Kenya. There we spent some time in conversation with a woman from South Sudan. She was taken away by a seventy-five-year-old man, when she was fourteen years old just because her father owed this man money. This man was beyond the age of sexual potency, so she was given to his son, who then sold her to others.

Eventually, she escaped, but during her long journey to the Kakuma Refugee Camp, she was raped by opposing militia.

It is heartbreaking to hear the cries of women like this.

In the Genesis 16 narrative, Hagar is driven out by her mistress, Sarah. A pregnant slave girl wanders in the wilderness, but the Lord hears her cries. The angel of the Lord appears to her. The narrative goes on to underline that this is the same angel of the Lord who appeared to Abraham in Genesis 22, when he was about to sacrifice his son Isaac (Gen 22:11, 15). It is the same angel of the Lord who appeared to Moses in the burning bush and commissioned him to save Israel (Exod 3:2). This is the Lord himself. However, before this angel of the Lord appeared to the great patriarchs, Abraham and Moses, he appeared to a black slave girl, Hagar.

This is powerful!

This angel of the Lord, it becomes clear, is God himself, in all these narratives. The angel of the Lord says to Hagar:

> "I will so greatly multiply your offspring that they cannot be counted for multitude." And the angel of the LORD said to her, "Now you have conceived and shall bear a son; you shall call him Ishmael, for the LORD has given heed to your affliction. (Gen 16:10–11 NRSV)

The Lord again hears the #MeToo cries of affliction from a woman. This time it is a black slave girl. Hagar acknowledges this God with potent words, "*Lahai-Roi*." He is a God who sees the suffering of #MeToo women. She names her son *Ishmael*, as he will always remind her of the God who hears the cries of #MeToo women.

Abraham and Sarah, however, have not seen the significance of this revelation of God through a slave woman. Sarah again banishes Hagar, this time with her young son, Ishmael. Why does Sarah banish Hagar and Ishmael into the wilderness? Most English translations, again, miss the point. Here are a few examples.

> "Sarah saw that the son whom Hagar the Egyptian had borne to Abraham was mocking." (Gen 21:9 NIV)

> "But Sarah saw Ishmael—the son of Abraham and her Egyptian servant Hagar—making fun of her son, Isaac. (NLT)

> "But Sarah noticed the son of Hagar the Egyptian—the son whom Hagar had borne to Abraham—mocking." (NET Bible)

These English translations make it seem like Sarah was right to be angry. How dare the slave lad make fun of the legitimate lad, Isaac!

The Hebrew word which is usually translated as "mocking" is *tsachak*. It is related to the name of her son Isaac (*Yitzchak*). Sarah did not like it that this slave boy was laughing or having fun with her son *Yitschak*. That was only the prerogative of the slave owners and their children. Half-breeds like Ishmael did not have the right to have fun, or live a good life. So she had them both banished as refugees into the wilderness.

Much of the refugee problem today is related to this issue of laughing or having fun or living a good life. Dominant groups, usually racially pure groups, never want subservient groups to prosper or be happy. Therefore, horrible things like rape and violence are brought upon them so that they are forced to flee as refugees. One such group are the Rohingyas of Burma. Burma is primarily a Buddhist country. The Rohingyas are considered to be lower-level people, who are also Muslim, therefore they are chased out by the Burmese Buddhist armies and the women and girls are raped by the Buddhist men. All of this takes places because the Burmese Buddhists cannot stand to see the Rohingyas live a normal life among them.

In the Genesis 21 narrative, God breaks through once again. After wandering around in the wilderness for several days, Hagar and Ishmael do not find any water. She leaves him under a bush, to die. "I do not want to see my child die in front of my eyes" she exclaims (Gen 21:16). Then she lifts her voice and weeps bitterly. In Hebrew this is the sound of hopeless and uncontrollable grief, a sound I heard so many times in the slum where I was reared, and a sound I heard in the wilderness of Kakuma, from the female refugees.

Right in the midst of this hopelessness, God breaks though. The narrative says,

> And God heard the voice of the boy; and the Angel of God called to Hagar from heaven, and said to her, "What troubles you, Hagar? Do not be afraid; for God has heard the voice of the boy where he is. Come, lift up the boy and hold him fast with your hand, for I will make a great nation of him." Then God opened her eyes and she saw a well of water. She went, and filled the skin with water, and gave the boy a drink. God was with the boy, and he grew up; he lived in the wilderness. (Gen 21:17–20 NRSV)

God heard the #MeToo cries of the slave girl and her slave half-breed son.

One of the methods of war we have noted is the rape of the girls of the opposing people. This happens a lot, even today. The Janjaweed are Arab militia in Sudan. An intrinsic part of their strategy was to rape South Sudanese African girls. The kids that were born to these girls who were raped were considered to be half-breeds. They are neither accepted by the Arabs or the South Sudanese Africans. I saw a similar awful scenario in the Democratic Republic of Congo. Warring militia would rape the girls of opposing militia. The girls then, who were carrying the babies of the opposing militia, were thrown out of their houses by their own parents, just because they were carrying the babies of the opposing militia. These girls had nowhere to go. Their children, the half-breeds, also had no place in society since they looked too much like the enemy militia.

During the time of Jesus, the half-breeds had no choice but to form their own communities. They were called the Samaritans. The Samaritans were the progeny of many decades of the rape of low-class Jewish girls. This happened under waves of invading armies—the Assyrians, the Babylonians, the Persians, the Greeks, the Romans, and so on. Each of these invading armies raped girls. I call these the Marys of the Bible. Their progeny were called the Samaritans. They were hated by the pure Jewish groups, and also the pure Romans, etc., yet Jesus constantly reached out to them. He talked about their virtues, like the Good Samaritan, who provided for the high-class Sadducee, even though the Sadducees hated them (Luke 10:25–37). Jesus talked about their life of faith, like the faithfulness of the Samaritan leper who was healed (Luke 17:11–19). In John 4, Jesus goes specifically to a Samaritan village to encounter a Samaritan woman. Jewish people always skirted around Samaritan villages since it would desecrate them. Jesus asked this Samaritan woman to give him a cup of water in her Samaritan cup, something a Jewish person would never do since this would desecrate him. Jesus sought to heal her from the sexual and emotional trauma she had experienced at the hands of six men. Jesus stresses that when half-breed women are abused by high-class people, and people in power, they are also raped and abused by their own men.

Jesus heard the #MeToo cries of the Samaritan woman, just like the angel of the LORD heard the #MeToo cries of Hagar and her half-breed son.

The Bible makes it clear that the same God hears the #MeToo cries of women and their half-breed children across the world, even today!

7

Miriam, the Sister of Moses, and the #MeToo Movement

The name Miriam is derived from the word *marah* which, as we have seen previously, means bitter. This bitterness was seen in the lives of several women in the Bible. 1 Samuel 1:10 describes the condition of Hannah, the mother of Samuel, who was not able to bear children and therefore lived a very bitter life: "She was in deep bitterness (*marah*) and so she prayed and wept bitterly." Infertility in the ancient world, and even today in so many parts of the world, is a cause of much bitterness for women. Women endure much scorn and injustice when they are unable to bear children.

Moses' sister's name was Miriam, "the Bitter One." She represented all that the Israelite women went through during the time of Egyptian slavery. The raping of girls and boys was a religiously sanctioned method of subjugation of people groups by the dominant culture in the ancient Near East. In the Sumerian religion, for example, raping the women they had conquered was based on the rape of Ninlil by the god Enlil, who accosts her and rapes her.

In the Greco-Roman world, Kathy Gaca has shown that the Roman soldiers followed a tripartite division of *gunaikes, parthenoi,* and *paides,* young women, virgins, and boys or girls. These were raped as a method of subjugating the areas they had conquered.[30] Other research has shown

30. Gaca, "Martial Rape, Pulsating Fear," 303–357; Gaca, "Ancient Warfare"; Gordon and Washington, "Rape as a Military Metaphor"; Camp and Fontaine, *Women, War, and Metaphor.*

that this kind of sexual violence against girls, boys, and women, which was carried out by ancient conquering kingdoms, carries on in modern times.[31]

Miriam's song gives some great insight into the horror that she and all the women of Israel experienced in Egypt. Exodus 15:20–21 reads,

> Then Miriam the prophet, Aaron's sister, took a timbrel in her hand, and all the women followed her, with timbrels and dancing. Miriam sang to them: "Sing to the LORD, for he is highly exalted. Both horse and driver he has hurled into the sea." (NIV)

The "horse and the driver," were not merely the animal and the human rider. The Egyptian god *Set* has the image of a horse's head and a pharaoh's body. This was the warrior pharaoh god. This was also the god who was responsible for the enslavement of other people groups, including the rape of women. Therefore, Miriam's song was a defiant song which praised the Lord for his victory over the pantheon of Egyptian gods, especially *Set*.

BITTER (MARAH) WATER

Immediately following the great miracle of their deliverance from the pharaoh and the gods of Egypt, the now free people encountered their first crisis: a lack of water. They did not have water for three days. Whenever there is a crisis of this kind, usually it is the most vulnerable in society that suffer—women and children. A lack of water is still a huge crisis in much of the world. Much injustice in Asia and Africa against women revolves around the scarcity of water. Women are the ones who carry water on their heads on flimsy clay jars for miles, and they are the ones who are assaulted by the evil men who prey on them. Girls do not go to school because they are the ones who have to get the water. Women are the ones who have to bear the consequences of water-borne diseases, from which their kids suffer and die: diseases like diarrhea, cholera, typhoid, and numerous other parasitic infections. The problems related to water—and its impact on women—must be multiplied manyfold when looking at ancient times.

Biblical narratives are crafted very carefully. Many times we miss the turning points because it is difficult to see them in the English translations. Immediately following Miriam, the Bitter One's song, the people of Israel encounter the water of *Marah*, "bitterness." The narrative says, "When they

---

31. Heineman, *Sexual Violence in Conflict Zones*; Smith, "Genocide and the Politics of Rape"; Camp and Fontaine, *Women, War, and Metaphor*.

came to *Marah*, they would not drink the water of *Marah* because it was bitter (*Marah*); therefore, it was called Marah" (Exod 15:23)

The word *marah* is repeated four times in this one verse. From a biblical perspective, whenever a word is repeated so many times, it is very important. In this case, the people were just displaying extreme and foolish thanklessness. If one does not have water for three days, one will drink any kind of water. There is a proverb in the Bible which says, "For one who is hungry everything bitter (*marah*) tastes sweet (*mathoq*)" (Prov 27:7). Besides this, the people were told that they should ingest "bitter" (*marah*) food and drink so that they always remember the bitterness of slavery (Exod 12:8). This must especially happen at the Passover commemoration. Sadly, in the history of the people of Israel, the only time this happens is during the time of Nehemiah, in the postexilic time (Neh 9:11).

What follows is rather mystical. The Lord asks Moses to throw an *etz*, tree, into the water, and after he does so, the water is healed. God then proclaims to them, "I am the Lord your healer (*rapha*)" (Exod 15:23). This miracle is replicated later by Elisha who says, "Thus says the LORD, I have healed (*rapha*) the water, from now on neither death nor miscarriage shall come from it" (2 Kgs 2:21). The diseases which were given to the Egyptians, including the turning of the water of the Nile into blood, were related to the religions of Egypt. These were the religions that became the basis of evil and injustice done to others in Egypt. So God promises them that if they do not practice these kinds of religions, which cause evil and injustice, then they will not have to endure the kinds of diseases that the Egyptians endured.

The obvious question is, "Can bitterness be changed to sweetness?" The biblical answer is "Yes." God can do miracles; however, his people need to always be ready to drink bitterness, to truly understand the needs of those who are in any bitterness.

MIRIAM AND HER MIDIANITE BEDOUIN BLACK SISTER-IN-LAW: SARAH AND HER BLACK EGYPTIAN SLAVE GIRL

Unfortunately, this same Miriam, the Bitter One, comes out against another woman. This time it is the black woman (*HaCushit*) Moses had married. The text repeats this twice, "For Moses had married an African Black woman (Num 12:1; my translation). She and Aaron questioned Moses' authority saying, "Do you think you are the only one with whom the Lord speaks? He has spoken to us as well" (Num 12:2; my translation). The Lord did not take kindly to this revolt against Moses by his sister Miriam, especially a revolt which was based on the race of her sister-in-law. Miriam, the Bitter One, should have known better because her own bitter experiences in Egypt were based on race. Her people were considered to be a detestable, disgusting, and abhorrent race in the eyes of the people of Egypt (Gen 46:33–34). It is because of this racial attitude that they were able to do horrible things against the people of Israel, including raping women and genocide (Exod 1).

It is a curious phenomenon. How is it that women who have experienced horrible bitterness and pain then turn around to discriminate against other women, especially when it comes to race? This is especially true when these women come into a place of power, as is the case with Miriam,

This phenomenon may be observed in a lot of modern-day situations. Those groups and tribes which have been marginalized and treated unjustly by dominant cultures often turn around and promulgate the same kinds of evils and injustices against others. Do these societies and individuals think this will help alleviate what they have suffered? Perhaps. However, this biblical narrative makes it clear that when one suffers at the hand of others, it should surely be an impetus to help lower groups of people and individuals. In this assistance, there is catharsis and healing.

The punishment of Miriam is telling, because it gets to the root of the racial injustice situation in this narrative. "Miriam became leprous like snow" (Num 12:10; cf. Isa 1:18). It also becomes clear that this racially oriented revolt was not led by Aaron, since he did not have the same consequence. It is as if God was saying to Miriam, "You want white, I will give you white." Unfortunately, this kind of whiteness was also a negative kind of whiteness; it was leprosy, the scariest kind of disease, and it caused her to become an outcast in society.

Another narrative which mirrors that of Miriam and Zipporah is the narrative of Sarai and Hagar in Genesis 16, which we have noted in the last chapter. Sarai was barren, which is a very sad situation in the ancient world. It is a hard situation, even today. However, Sarai was a woman of wealth and she had slave girls (*shiphkah*). Egyptian documents give us the knowledge that these were black girls from upper Egypt, i.e. from further south into Africa. Because Hagar was a black slave girl, Sarai had the power to have her sleep with her husband, Abram. This was just accepted of slave girls from Africa. However, when Hagar conceived, Sarai became jealous and infuriated, so she humiliated Hagar. In the ancient world, this humiliation is associated with the lower class of society to which Hagar belonged. Many times it took the form of flogging, when the slave was naked. Hagar fled. She reached a well, where the angel of the Lord encountered her. This raises Hagar's status to that of a prophetess. The angel of the Lord in the Hebrew Bible is God himself. God appears to prophets like Abraham and Moses. However, here he appears to Hagar. This is elevating her status a million times, and giving her justice for all the injustices she has endured. "She called the name of the LORD, who spoke to her, 'A God who sees,'" (Gen 16:13). She expressed the faith that this God always looks out for the weak and the marginalized.

The same story is repeated in Genesis 21. This time Sarah has a son, and calls his name Isaac (*Yitzchak*), "the Laughable One." The narrative says, "The child grew and was weaned" (Gen 21:8). The Hebrew word here, *gamal*, refers to a boy who has ripened to the age of becoming a man, a bar mitzvah, perhaps twelve years old. At his coming-of-age ceremony, Abraham made a great feast (Gen 21:8). The next verse is often translated as "Sarah saw the son of the slave girl, mocking Isaac." Literally, he was *yitzkhaking*, he was having fun. It is a play on words on the name Isaac (*Yitzchak*). However, again Sarah got infuriated and threw the slave girl out.

Contempt for the weak and marginalized is historically directed by high-class males toward low-class women and girls. However, there have been many instances when high-class women have enacted racial injustices and evil against low-class women whom they consider to be racially inferior.

Thankfully, again, the Lord appears to Hagar in the wilderness and rescues her and her young son. This is indeed what the prophet Isaiah proclaimed,

> The poor and needy search for water,
> but there is none;
> their tongues are parched with thirst.
> But I the Lord will answer them;
> I, the God of Israel, will not forsake them.
> I will make rivers flow on barren heights,
> and springs within the valleys.
> I will turn the desert into pools of water,
> and the parched ground into springs.
> I will put in the desert
> the cedar and the acacia, the myrtle and the olive.

I will set junipers in the wasteland,
the fir and the cypress together,
so that people may see and know,
may consider and understand,
that the hand of the Lord has done this,
that the Holy One of Israel has created it. (Isa 41:17–20)

Moses, in contrast to Miriam, his sister, is called "a very meek (`anavi)` person" (Num 12:3). This is a person who is spiritually, emotionally, and socially poor. The prophets use this word several times to describe people who are poor because of the systems of injustice they have had to endure. Isaiah the prophet, for example, talks about the mission of the Messiah. "The Spirit of the Sovereign LORD is on me, because the LORD has anointed me to proclaim good news to the poor (`Anavim)`" (Isa 61:1 NIV). And Amos constantly rebukes the people for unjust things that are doing to the `anavim` (Amos 2:7; 8:4).

Moses, it seems clear, intentionally sought to become poor, to live with the poor and those who were more despised than even his own people, the Israelites. He lived this out so much that he decided to marry a black woman—something that was completely unheard of in his society. Throughout the Bible, this is the model—becoming poor and needy in order to better understand and communicate with the poor and needy. This is the virtue of the God of the Bible, and so must this be the virtue of the people who seek to follow him.

This same "poor" Moses cries out to God to have mercy on his sister, to forgive her racial sin. He cries to the Lord in great anguish (tsa'aq), "Please heal her" (Num 12:13). The Hebrew word for "healing" (rapha') is quite a complex word. It describes social, mental, psychological, spiritual, and racial healing. In many senses, this is the answer to injustice and racial prejudice in society. Only this kind of holistic healing can bring about reconciliation in global society.

Reconciliation, however, also means repentance. So, Mary had to remain outside the community for seven days. She had to acknowledge the harm that she had done to society because of her racial sin. It should be also noted that the community stayed with her, as she acknowledged her racial sin. After seven days of penance, they all moved on to the next stage of their journey.

Miriam was healed. However, she had to spend seven days outside the camp. This was the place of restorative justice. The Torah prescribes that reconciliation happened through the sacrificial system, reconciliation to God and reconciliation to society outside the camp. This was a clean place (e.g. Lev 4:12; Exod 29:14). When the community needed cleansing, this always happened "outside the camp" (Num 19:3, 9). The space outside the camp was the space for healing with respect to several diseases, including leprosy (Lev 14:3). This is the space where the presence of God dwelt in the Tent of Meeting, and anyone who sought to encounter the Lord had to go "outside the camp" (Exod 33:7). Interpreting these kinds of texts from the Torah, the New Testament exhorts Christians, "Let us, then, go to him outside the camp, bearing the disgrace he bore" (Heb 13:13 NIV). Jesus was crucified outside the camp, just like the sacrificial system in the Torah prescribed. This is the most important place, the place of reconciliation between God and humanity, and reconciliation among humanity.

Miriam, the Bitter One, experienced physical, racial, emotional, and spiritual healing at this place of encounter outside the camp. Outside the camp is the place where individuals would encounter other individuals, who would counsel them toward healing. Outside the camp is the place where they would have time to think about what they had done wrong. It seems clear that this system of justice is much better than the modern prison system.

8

Mary, the Mother of Jesus, and the #MeToo Movement

The narrative of Jesus the Messiah of Israel and the world, and of Mary, the mother of Jesus, picks up many, many years later.

The narrative of Tamar and the matriarchs and patriarchs of Israel is set around the twentieth century BC, perhaps 2000–1700 BC. This is followed by the enslavement of the children of Israel by very cruel Egyptian pharaohs. Miriam (Mary), the sister of Moses, comes from this period, though scholars disagree on the exact dates. Much depends on proving who was the cruelest of the pharaohs. Was it Ramesses II (1279–1213 BC)? Or Thutmoses III (1485–1431 BC)? The list goes on. The narrative of Rahab also belongs to this period of time. The narrative of Bathsheba, the wife of Uriah, comes from around 1000 BC.

The period of united monarchy under David and Solomon is followed be several years of injustice against the poor, the widows, the orphans, and the foreigners. The prophets and the psalms warn against these horrible forms of injustice and evil. Here are a few examples:

> "Your New Moon feasts and your appointed festivals I hate with all my being. They have become a burden to me; I am weary of bearing them. When you spread out your hands in prayer, I hide my eyes from you; even when you offer many prayers, I am not listening. Your hands are full of blood! Wash and make yourselves clean. Take your evil deeds out of my sight; stop doing wrong. Learn to

do right; seek justice. Defend the oppressed. Take up the cause of the fatherless; plead the case of the widow." (Isa 1:14–17 NIV)

"This is what the LORD says: "Go down to the palace of the king of Judah and proclaim this message there: 'Hear the word of the LORD to you, king of Judah, you who sit on David's throne—you, your officials and your people who come through these gates. This is what the LORD says: Do what is just and right. Rescue from the hand of the oppressor the one who has been robbed. Do no wrong or violence to the foreigner, the fatherless or the widow, and do not shed innocent blood in this place." (Jer 22:1–3 NIV)

"I will send my messenger, who will prepare the way before me. Then suddenly the Lord you are seeking will come to his temple; the messenger of the covenant, whom you desire, will come," says the LORD Almighty. But who can endure the day of his coming? Who can stand when he appears? For he will be like a refiner's fire or a launderer's soap. He will sit as a refiner and purifier of silver; he will purify the Levites and refine them like gold and silver. Then the LORD will have men who will bring offerings in righteousness, and the offerings of Judah and Jerusalem will be acceptable to the LORD, as in days gone by, as in former years. "So, I will come to put you on trial. I will be quick to testify against sorcerers, adulterers and perjurers, against those who defraud laborers of their wages, who oppress the widows and the fatherless, and deprive the foreigners among you of justice, but do not fear me," says the LORD Almighty. (Mal 3:1–5 NIV)

A father to the fatherless, a defender of widows, is God in his holy dwelling. (Ps 68:5 NIV)

Blessed are those whose help is the God of Jacob,
whose hope is in the LORD their God.
He is the Maker of heaven and earth, the sea, and everything in them—
he remains faithful forever.
He upholds the cause of the oppressed and gives food to the hungry.
The LORD sets prisoners free,
The LORD gives sight to the blind,
The LORD lifts up those who are bowed down, the LORD loves the
    righteous.
The LORD watches over the foreigner and sustains the fatherless and the
    widow, but he frustrates the ways of the wicked.
The LORD reigns forever, your God, O Zion, for all generations.
Praise the LORD." (Ps 146:5–10 NIV)

Sadly, the people who were once enslaved and raped now practice the same injustices and evil against the poor, the widows, the orphans, and the foreigners. The very last section of the Hebrew Bible is 2 Chronicles 36:11–23. The following section is poignant. Significantly, it comes from the conclusion of the Hebrew Bible.[32] This conclusion underlines the main reason behind the final punishment of Israel and Judah.

> Furthermore, all the leaders of the priests and the people became more and more unfaithful, following all the detestable practices of the nations and defiling the temple of the LORD, which he had consecrated in Jerusalem. The LORD, the God of their ancestors, sent word to them through his messengers again and again, because he had pity on his people and on his dwelling place. But they mocked God's messengers, despised his words and scoffed at his prophets until the wrath of the LORD was aroused against his people and there was no remedy. (2 Chr 36:14–16 NIV)

This section makes it clear that both the kingdoms—Judah, the Southern Kingdom, and Israel, the Northern Kingdom—are destroyed because of these injustices. The Northern Kingdom was captured and destroyed by the Assyrians in 722 BC. The Southern Kingdom was captured and destroyed in 587–586 BC.

Archeological material from the reigns of Neo-Assyrian kings Shalmaneser III (858–824 BC); Tiglath-Pileser III (744–727 BC); Shalmaneser V (726–722 BC); Sargon II (721–705 BC); Sennacherib (704–681 BC), etc., makes it clear that these were very cruel kings. Here are a couple of quotes:

> "With their blood, I dyed the mountains red like red wool . . . I carried off captives [and] possessions from them . . . raped their adolescent boys and girls."[33]

The enslavement of women, brutal massacres, and raping boys and girls were very common strategies of war practiced by Neo-Assyrian, Babylonian, Persian, Greek, and Roman kingdoms.[34] Much of the records

---

32. It may be noted that while the Book of Malachi is the last book of the English Old Testament, the Book of Chronicles is the last book of the Hebrew Bible. This is a significant difference, to understand the main import of the Hebrew Bible.

33. Grayson, *Assyrian Royal Inscriptions, Part 2*, 126–27.

34. It may be noted that this war strategy is seen in several global internal wars even today. The raping of Bangladeshi women and boys by Pakistani soldiers in 1970–71 has been widely reported. So is the raping of black Sudanese women by the Arab Sudanese and the Janjaweed forces.

show that these rapes were carried out so that the conquering armies could maintain perpetual control over the conquered people's groups.

The Case of the Samaritans

The Samaritans were a people of mixed race. When the Assyrians (and later the Babylonians) captured Israel and then Judea, they took the high classes of society into exile. Those from the lower classes of people (`am ha-aretz)—the poor, widows, orphans, foreigners, etc.—were left behind to be raped by the Assyrian and Babylonian soldiers. They were also forced to marry other low-class people who were brought into Israel from other territories captured by the Assyrians, the Babylonians, and the Persians. The mixed races was a war strategy to make sure that subsequent generations were not pure races, and so that they would remain in perpetual subjugation.

In 2 Chronicles 36:22–23, when Cyrus the Persian emperor allowed the high-class Judeans to return from the exile they encountered the `am ha-Aretz, the low-class people of the land. These were the Samaritans—the mixed races. These were the progeny of low-class women who were left behind by the victorious Assyrians and Babylonians, and who were raped by successive bands of invading forces. From that time on, there was tension between the high-class returnees, also called the Judeans, and the `am ha-aretz, or the low-class people, the Samaritans.[35] Sadly, this was the state of affairs during the time of the birth of Jesus the Messiah. Joseph and Mary came from Nazareth, in the north, and this territory was populated by the `am ha-aretz.

Jesus was born during the time of the Greco-Roman occupation of Israel. The Greco-Roman practice of populace-raping warfare was far more severe than the previous Assyrian, Babylonian, and Persian empires. *Diarpazein* was the war method of capturing girls and boys (παῖδες), virgins (παρθένοι), and women (γυναῖκες), and taking them as sexual slaves.[36] This was done after all the fighting-age males were killed. This was also done so that the mixed-race kids who were born would remain as their subjects and slaves.

It is in this horrible context for girls, boys and women that the New Testament applies the words of Isaiah 7:14 to Mary, "The virgin (*Parthenos*)

---

35. Several scholars have written about this phenomenon. Notable among these is Lawrence Schiffman, *From Text to Tradition.*

36. Gaca, "Martial Rape, Pulsating Fear," 303–57.

will conceive and give birth to a son, and they will call him Immanuel" (which means "God with us") (Matt 1:23 NIV). Virgins were always taken away by the Roman soldiers as sexual slaves. However, miraculously, one virgin remained a virgin, and she was found to be with a child of the Holy Spirit. And, so Joseph was asked to take Mary (the Bitter One) as his wife. She was a virgin. She was providentially untouched by a Roman soldier.

Another question which is often asked by scholars is, "Why is the name Mary such a common name during the time of the birth of Jesus?" Obviously, the ʾam ha-aretz knew that the name Mary meant "the Bitter One." The Gospels note that the women who were present at the crucifixion of Jesus were all named Mary, "Many women . . . who had followed Jesus from Galilee, ministering to him, among whom were Mary Magdalene, and Mary the mother of James and Joseph, and the mother of the sons of Zebedee" (Matt 27:55–56; Mark 15:40; Luke 23:49; John 19:25). The women who assisted in the burial of Jesus also were all named Mary (Matt 27:61; Mark 15:47; Luke 23:55). And the women who ran to finish the anointing work on the third day, (i.e., the first day of the week) were also all named Mary (Matt 28:1; Mark 16:1; Luke 24:10; John 20:1).

It seems like the Gospels are saying that all the people who encountered the deepest suffering of the Messiah Jesus were not his disciples. They all ran away. Instead, it was all of the Marys. It seems clear that Mary was a common name because when a little baby girl was born, the parents looked at this little baby, and said, "I am so sorry you were born. Your life will be Marah. You are Mary!"

Yet, the New Testament underlines that it was not the "who's who" of society who were with Jesus at his deepest time of grief and sorrow. It was not the disciples, with whom Jesus had spent so much of his brief ministry. Not too long before that time, actually, they had gone to sleep, during his deep period of agony at the garden of Gethsemane (Matt 26:36–46; Mark 14:32–42; Luke 22:39–46; John 18:1).

It was the women—all of whom were named Mary, "the Bitter One." Quite telling!

THIS CHILD IS DIFFERENT

The Greek text of the genealogy of Jesus the Messiah, the Son of David, the Son of Abraham (Matt 1:1), makes it clear that the birth of Jesus is not like the birth of his predecessors. In the case of the birth of the others, it says, "so and so *egennesen* so and so; so and so fathered so and so." Only in the case of Jesus, the text says, "The birth of Jesus the Messiah happened this way. His mother Mary was betrothed to Joseph, but before they came together in marital and sexual union, she was found to be pregnant through the Holy Spirit" (Matt 1:18). This is like no other birth.

It goes on, "But because Joseph, her husband, was a just person, and because he did not want to bring shame on her, he resolved to send her away privately." (Matt 1:19). In an honor-and-shame-based society, this was an honorable thing to do.

Joseph knew what the Roman soldiers did to virgins in his area. But he was a just person, unlike the other men we have encountered in the four other narratives of Tamar, Rahab, Ruth, and the wife of Uriah. In calling him a just person, the narrative compared him to another person in the Torah: Noah (Gen 6:9).

English translations say, "he had in mind to divorce her quietly." The Greek word *apoluo*, is a very gentle word, i.e., "setting her aside," or better still "forgive her," just like the master in Matthew 18:27 "releases" the servant and "forgives the debts" of the servant.

Joseph was the new Boaz. He was the *Chayil*, the spiritually, emotionally, physically, strong person.

THE NAME YESHUA

Knowing the virtues of this good man, the angel of the Lord appears to Joseph in a dream and says to him,

> Joseph son of David, do not be afraid to take Mary home as your wife, because what is conceived in her is from the Holy Spirit. She will give birth to a son, and you are to give him the name Jesus, because he will save his people from their sins. (Matt 1:20, 21 NIV)

The question is, "What sins?"

The narratives of the four women we have covered thus far describe the nature of the sins. It is personal sins of the kind done by Judah (Gen 38); the men of Jericho (Josh 2); David (2 Sam 11); and the sons of Naomi and Elimelech (Ruth 1). These sins are based on the religious, social, racial, etc. norms of the day, and yet these are deeply personal sins. These people blatantly went against the teachings of the Torah, and against common sense. They used the norms of their day to do evil against the weak and the vulnerable, especially women. These narratives also make it clear that "sins" are much deeper than personal sins. Sins are deeply ingrained in the deep systems of society. It is what people do or say without even thinking. It is what people do or say or think without calling it sin. It is much more than personal sins; it is systemic evil and injustices that are typically done against the weak, the vulnerable, and the marginalized of society. It is contempt for the weak and the marginalized which enables people to do evil against another person or group of people, without thinking it is a sin.

"Do not be afraid to take Mary as your wife."

Mary, the Bitter One, in many ways is emblematic of all the Marys of the Bible and the world. Her life, no doubt, has been bitter. Just like the Miriam of the Torah, and Tamar, and Rahab, and Ruth, and the wife of Uriah, she has also experienced much bitterness. Joseph is reminded to be the new Boaz and Joshua.

"You shall call his name Jesus, for he shall save his people from their sins."

Jesus is the Son of David. Yet, he is not the victorious and proud king who looked on Uriah and Bathsheba with disdain, and then raped her. Much in contrast to this picture, he is the humble king who said, "Take my yoke upon you and learn from me, for I am gentle and humble in heart" (Matt 11:29 NIV). He is just (*Tsadiq*), salvation (*Yeshua*), poor (`*ani*), and "mounted on a donkey, on a colt, the foal of a donkey" (Zech 9:9; Matt 21:2, 5, 7).

His Name, His Very Being and Nature, is Yeshua.

This is what the word "name" means in the Bible. In the Western context, people give names for all sorts of reasons. In my classes, I ask my students on the very first day, "What does your name mean?" The usual answers are "I do not know" or "My mother saw this movie, and she liked the name of the actress/character" and so on. In the Bible a name is rather profound. It defines the identity of the person. So, for example, in Genesis 32, Jacob (*Ya'aqov*, "the heel" or "deceptive one") is running away from a series of deceptions. He has deceived his father, his brother, Esau, his own wives, his father-in-law, and the list goes on. But not only does he deceive others, he is also deceived by others. In Genesis 32, he (*Ya'aqov*) wrestles with (*Ya'aveq*) God at the ford of Jabbok (*Ya'avoq*). In English, we miss the whole point. However, in the original Hebrew, there is a whole lot of play on words.

Essentially, God is shaking up Jacob from the inside out, i.e., God is wrestling (*Ya'aveq*) with Jacob's inner being, his name (*Ya'aqov*) at this place of encounter called *Ya'avoq*. Finally, God asks him, "What is your name?" He says, "*Ya'aqov*," or "the heel." God says to him, "Your name will no longer be Jacob (*Ya'aqov*), but Israel (*Yisra'el*), because you have struggled (*sarah*) with God and with humans and have overcome" (Gen 32:28 NIV). When God changed the name of Jacob, to Yisra'el, he completely transformed his identity.

Another example in the Hebrew Bible is the name of God. When Moses encountered God in the burning bush in the wilderness, God said to him,

> "I am the God of your father, the God of Abraham, the God of Isaac and the God of Jacob." At this, Moses hid his face, because he was afraid to look at God. The LORD said, "I have indeed seen the misery of my people in Egypt. I have heard them crying out because of their slave drivers, and I am concerned about their suffering. So, I have come down to rescue them from the hand of the Egyptians." (Exod 3:6–8 NIV)

God says that he will accomplish this task through Moses. Moses' next question is, "Suppose I go to the Israelites and say to them, 'The God of your fathers has sent me to you,' and they ask me, 'What is his name?' Then what shall I tell them" (Exod 3:13 NIV)? To this God responds,

> "'I AM WHO I AM (*EHYEH ASHER EHYEH*).' This is what you are to say to the Israelites: 'I AM has sent me to you.'" God also said to Moses, 'Say to the Israelites, "The LORD, the God of your fathers—the God of Abraham, the God of Isaac and the God of Jacob—has sent me to you." This is my name forever, the name you shall call me from generation to generation." (Exod 3:14–15 NIV)

The four-letter name of God, *YHWH*, comes from this phrase, I AM THAT I AM. He is the BEING. He is the BEING from whom all "being" derives. He is the source of all that there is. This is the name of God.

There are scores of illustrations in the Bible, regarding the significance of one's name. For this reason, the angel of the Lord says to Joseph, "His name shall be called *Yeshua*!"

WHO IS YESHUA IN THE HEBREW BIBLE?

The book of Genesis ends at the point where the children of Israel are going to be enslaved for 400 years. Yet, the last song ends with the longing that the people will see the salvation (*Yeshua*) of the Lord (Gen 49:18). In Exodus 2:17, when Moses protects the daughters of Jethro, the priest of the Medianites, from the hands of the men who were harassing them, he is called a *Yeshua* (Exod 2:17). When pharaoh and his army of Egyptian deities are pursuing the children of Israel, a despondent group who have been enslaved for 400 years, Moses says to them—really against all hope— "Do not be afraid. Stand firm and you will see the salvation (*yeshua*) the LORD will bring you today. The Egyptians you see today you will never see again" (Exod 14:13). The same thought is expressed after this salvation. *Yeshua* is the Lord, YHWH, who saves the people from servitude to Egyptian gods and the pharaoh (Exod 15:2). In 1 Samuel 2, Hannah sings a song after she gives birth to her son Samuel, and then dedicates him to the Lord. She has for many years endured the scorn of men and women—especially women—because she has not been able to have a child. Barrenness was and is considered to be a huge curse, a symbol of weakness, and yet she prayed with many tears, and God answered her prayers. So, she sings a song of thanksgiving to God, "Then Hannah prayed and said: 'My heart rejoices in the LORD; in the LORD my horn is lifted high. My mouth boasts over my enemies, for I delight in your deliverance (*Yeshua*)" (1 Sam 2:1 NIV). Similarly, toward the end of his reign, a very repentant David exclaims, "Sing to the LORD, all the earth; proclaim his salvation (*Yeshua*) day after day" (1 Chr 16:23 NIV). This *Yeshua*, or salvation, is not just for the children of Israel. It is meant for the whole earth—all the races and all of creation.

The Psalms of Lament constantly express the hope of seeing the *Yeshua*, the salvation of God (Ps 3:3; 13:6; 14:7; 21:2; 22:1; 42:6, 12; 69:30; and so on). These psalms express much despair about the injustice toward the weak and the marginalized. Some of these injustices are physical, some are political, some are economic, some are social, and yet these psalms always end in the hope of seeing the *Yeshua*, the salvation of the Lord. Psalm 118 is a good example, "I will give you thanks, for you answered me; you have become my salvation," (Ps 118:21 NIV; also 118:14, 15) or Psalm 69:29, "But as for me, afflicted and in pain—may your salvation (*Yeshua*), O God, protect me. (Ps 69:29 NIV)

The prophet Isaiah constantly dwells on the *Yeshua* motif. Right in the midst of prophecies of judgment against the people for sins, evil, and injustices against the poor, orphans, widows, and strangers (Isaiah 6–12), he exclaims, "Surely God is my salvation (*Yeshua*); I will trust and not be afraid. The LORD, the LORD himself, is my strength and my defense; he has become my salvation (*Yeshua*)" (Isa 12:2 NIV). As the invading forces come, the prophet Isaiah and the people cry out, "LORD, be gracious to us; we long for you. Be our strength every morning, our salvation (*Yeshua*) in time of distress" (Isa 33:2 NIV). Right in the midst of destruction, the prophet Isaiah expresses the hope of a Messiah, "How beautiful on the mountains are the feet of those who bring good news, who proclaim peace, who bring good tidings, who proclaim *Yeshua*; who say to Zion, 'Your God reigns'" (Isa 52:7 NIV)! Again, right in the midst of exile and enslavement by the Babylonians, the prophet Isaiah declares,

> He saw that there was no one, he was appalled that there was no one to intervene; so, his own arm brought salvation (*Yeshua*) for him, and his own justice sustained him. He put on justice as his breastplate, and the helmet of salvation (*Yeshua*) on his head. (Isa 59:16–17a NIV)

It becomes clear the salvation (*Yeshua*) of the Lord is prophesied about throughout the book of Isaiah, in the context of much injustice done to the exiled, the weak, and the marginalized people of God. These are the poor, the widows, the orphans, and the foreigners now. It is in this context that the angel of the Lord says to Joseph, "You are to give him the name *Yeshua*, because he will save (*Yeshua*) his people from their sins" (Matt 1:21 NIV). The children of Israel sinned against the poor, the weak, the marginalized, the widows, the orphans, and the foreigners, and now for about 400 years, they themselves were the poor, the weak, the marginalized, the widows, the orphans, and the foreigners.

At the right time *Yeshua* came to *yeshua* them from this horrible situation.

THE VIRGIN MARY BEARS YESHUA

The meaning of Yeshua is most clearly seen in the prophet Isaiah, so it is no accident that Matthew actually quotes him, to underline this:

> "The virgin will conceive and give birth to a son, and they will call him Immanuel" (which means "God with us"). (Matt 1:23 NIV)

> Therefore, the Lord himself will give you a sign: The virgin will conceive and give birth to a son, and will call him Immanuel. (Isa 7:14 NIV)

It should be noted that Matthew wants to underline the Hebrew word *Immanuel,* to translate into Greek, this means "God with us." The text is making it clear that this Son was not an ordinary child, this was God, and this is what the prophet Isaiah intended.

Isaiah also called this a sign. The Hebrew word for "sign" is '*Ot*. Throughout the Hebrew Bible, this word is used to describe the presence of God and his awesomeness. Right at the beginning, Genesis 1:14, the planetary system and the cosmos is called the '*Ots*, or "signs of God." When God placed the rainbow in the sky to signify his gracious presence, he called it an '*Ot*, or "sign" (Gen 9:12–17). When God made a covenant with Abraham, he asked him and all later generations to be circumcised; this too was called an '*Ot* (Gen 17:11). All the miracles which God did to show the Egyptians that their gods were no match for YHWH, the God of the Bible, were called '*Ots* (Exod 4:8, 9, 28, 30; 7:3; 10:1–2; etc.). The blood of the Passover lamb on the doorposts, a symbol of the powerful presence of God, was also called an '*Ot* (Exod 13:9, 16). The Sabbath and all the special days of encounter with God were also called '*Ots* (Exod 31:13, 17). When the LORD gave the Torah to Moses at Mount Sinai, it was called the '*Ot*, (Deut 6:8, 22).

When Isaiah the prophet prophesied that the Lord himself will give you an '*Ot*, a "sign," he was declaring that this Son would be God himself breaking through into history and humanity, just like he did during the days of Moses.

The New Testament and the Greek translation of the Hebrew Bible uses the word *Parthenos*, or "virgin," to describe Mary. If Mary had not been a virgin, and if conception had come through normal intercourse between a man and a woman, this would not have been a divine sign. The Hebrew word *Ha-Almah* is used two other times in the Hebrew Bible; the first comes when Abraham's servant searches for a "virgin" who he could bring back to marry Isaac (Gen 24:43), and the second time it is used to describe Miriam, the Bitter One, the sister of Moses (Exod 2:8). The text obviously wants us to see the connection between the two Marys. By God's protective grace, both the Marys were virgins. The virgin birth of Jesus was very crucial. There was no doubt that this child was of the Holy Spirit, and therefore God. The Gospel of Luke gives more details. This time, the narrative is told from the perspective of Mary:

> In the sixth month of Elizabeth's pregnancy, God sent the angel Gabriel to Nazareth, a town in Galilee, to a virgin pledged to be married to a man named Joseph, a descendant of David. The virgin's name was Mary. The angel went to her and said, "Greetings, you who are highly favored! The Lord is with you." Mary was greatly troubled at his words and wondered what kind of greeting this might be. But the angel said to her, "Do not be afraid, Mary; you have found favor with God. You will conceive and give birth to a son, and you are to call him Jesus. He will be great and will be called the Son of the Most High. The Lord God will give him the throne of his father David, and he will reign over Jacob's descendants forever; his kingdom will never end." "How will this be," Mary asked the angel, "since I am a virgin?" The angel answered, "The Holy Spirit will come on you, and the power of the Most High will overshadow you. So, the holy one to be born will be called the Son of God. Even Elizabeth your relative is going to have a child in her old age, and she who was said to be unable to conceive is in her sixth month. For no word from God will ever fail." "I am the Lord's servant," Mary answered. "May your word to me be fulfilled." Then the angel left her. (Luke 1:26–38 NIV)

This narrative is a very powerful description of the faith and integrity of Mary, the Bitter One. The narrative uses the word *Parthenos*, or "virgin," to describe her three times, underscoring this miraculous divine protection of Mary.

The angel Gabriel's greeting to Mary clearly outlines the mission of her life. "*Chaire*, Rejoice, *keCharitomen*, one who is blessed by God's grace, the LORD is with you" (Luke 1:28). There is a play on words in both these terms. Instead of her name Mary, the Bitter One, she is called one who is full of divine grace and favor, and so she is the Rejoicing One. In a crucial messianic passage, the people of Israel are also told to "*Khaire*, Rejoice . . . Behold your king is coming to you; justice and salvation (*Yeshua*) is he" (Zech 9:9).

A perplexed Mary is then told that she will conceive and bear a son, "and you will name him Jesus (*Yeshua*)" (Luke 1:31). This is a very powerful statement because in ancient Near Eastern societies it is only the father that names the child. Here, Mary is told that she should name the child *Yeshua*, which of course is also the same message Joseph receives later.

Mary is then told, "He will be great and will be called the Son of the Most High. The Lord God will give him the throne of his father David" (Luke 1:32 NIV).

Mary responds, "How can this be, since I am a virgin?"

The angel then says to her, "The Holy Spirit will come on you, and the power of the Most High will overshadow you. So, the holy one to be born will be called the Son of God." (Luke 1:35 NIV)

The question is who is this Most High (*Hupistou*) who overshadows Mary? In Hebrew, the name is *El Elyon*. This is a very common name for God in the Psalms. For example: "I will give thanks to the LORD because of his righteousness; I will sing the praises of the name of the LORD Most High (Ps 7:17 NIV)"; "For the king trusts in the LORD; through the unfailing love of the Most High he will not be shaken (Ps 21:7 NIV)"; and in other places (Ps 13:5; 21:7; 106:11; etc.). Two gentile people are said to be worshippers of *El Elyon*, God Most High. These are Melchizedek, the King of Jerusalem, who engages with Abraham (Gen 14:18), and Balaam, who prophesies regarding the birth of the Messiah (Num 24:16).

Therefore, this son who is born of Mary is called the Son of God. The New Testament does not go into details, except to make it clear that this was a miracle. Mary, though perplexed, simply says, "Behold, I am the servant of the Lord; let it be to me according to your word" (Luke 1:38 ESV). This powerful and faith-filled response is similar to the responses of the other four *Eshet Chayil*: Tamar, Rahab, Ruth, and Bathsheba.

Following this, when Mary goes to visit her cousin, Elizabeth, the latter exclaims, "Blessed are you among women, and blessed is the child you will bear! But why am I so favored, that the mother of my Lord should come to me" (Luke 1:42–43 NIV)?

Mary is called the Blessed One. She is also called "mother of my LORD." In each of these, Mary is raised up to a very high level. This again, is quite similar to what Tamar, Rahab, and Ruth experienced.

MARY'S SONG

In response to Elizabeth's pronouncement, Mary also sings a song. In the liturgy, this song is called the *Magnificat*:

> "My soul glorifies the Lord
> And my spirit rejoices in God my Savior,
> For he has been mindful of the humble state of his servant.

From now on all generations will call me blessed,
For the Mighty One has done great things for me—holy is his name.
His mercy extends to those who fear him, from generation to generation.
He has performed mighty deeds with his arm; he has scattered those who are proud in their inmost thoughts.
He has brought down rulers from their thrones but has lifted up the humble.
He has filled the hungry with good things but has sent the rich away empty.
He has helped his servant Israel, remembering to be merciful
to Abraham and his descendants forever, just as he promised our ancestors." (Luke 1:46–55 NIV)

Mary's song has crucial parallels with Hannah's song in 1 Samuel 2. It is clear that both of these songs, coming from two different eras, express the heart cries of Marys throughout history.

Hannah's song is as follows:

"My heart rejoices in the LORD; in the LORD my horn is lifted high. My mouth boasts over my enemies, for I delight in your deliverance.

"There is no one holy like the LORD; there is no one besides you; there is no Rock like our God.

"Do not keep talking so proudly or let your mouth speak such arrogance, for the LORD is a God who knows, and by him deeds are weighed.

"The bows of the warriors are broken, but those who stumbled are armed with strength.

"Those who were full hire themselves out for food, but those who were hungry are hungry no more. She who was barren has borne seven children, but she who has had many sons pines away.

"The LORD brings death and makes alive; he brings down to the grave and raises up.

"The LORD sends poverty and wealth; he humbles and he exalts.

"He raises the poor from the dust and lifts the needy from the ash heap; he seats them with princes and has them inherit a throne of honor.

"For the foundations of the earth are the LORD's; on them he has set the world.

"He will guard the feet of his faithful servants, but the wicked will be silenced in the place of darkness.

"It is not by strength that one prevails; those who oppose the LORD will be broken.

"The Most High will thunder from heaven; the LORD will judge the ends of the earth. He will give strength to his king and exalt the horn of his anointed." (1 Sam 2:1–10 NIV)

The parallels between the songs of these two marginalized and unjustly treated women show the heart cry of Marys throughout history.

1. Despite their condition, both exult in the LORD (1 Sam 2:1; Luke 1:46).

2. Both rejoice in the salvation (*Yeshua*) of God (1 Sam 2:1; Luke 1:47). In many senses both of these are a show of defiance against their enemies, the people in power.

3. Both of them declare themselves to be the servants of God (1 Sam 1:11; Luke 1:48) The Hebrew word, *amah*, and Greek, *doulos*, are both negative words. These are used of sexual slaves of the Romans and Canaanites. In Luke 1:54, all of Israel is called *paidos*, a girl or boy who is used as a sexual slave by the Romans. However, when they are related to the God of the Bible, he protects them from injustice and harm.

4. Both of them warn the "proud and arrogant ones" (1 Sam 2:3; Luke 1:51). These people are the ones who did unjust things against the weak people of society. However, in these songs, both declare that the proud and the arrogant will be brought low.

5. Both of them call out the rich (Hebrew *asharim*; Greek *ploutos*) as a class that has become rich by doing unjust and evil things to the poor people. The poor are poor, because they have been unjustly treated by the rich and the rulers (1 Sam 2:7; Luke 1:53).

6. Both declare that the weak and humiliated people in society will be delivered from this state of humiliation (1 Sam 2:7–8; Luke 1:52). This cry for being rescued from the state of humiliation is a very deep one. The Greek word, *tapeinos*, is used of people who are physically, mentally, or socially raped (Exod 1:12; Deut 22:29; 26:7).

7. Both put their hope in justice (Hebrew *Tsdakah*; Greek *dikaios*) (1 Sam 2:2–3; Luke 1:53).

8. Both express the thought that the "weak" will be raised to the level of physical, emotional, economic, and spiritual strength, *Chayil*, just like Boaz and Joshua (1 Sam 2:4; Ruth 4:11; Luke 1:49).

9. Both claim that those who are hungry (Greek *peinao; ra'av*), are hungry because of systems of injustice that are pitted against them. These will experience "the good," (Greek *Agathos*) just as it was in Genesis 1 and 2 (1 Sam 2:5; Luke 1:53).

10. Both appeal to God's remembrance (Hebrew *zakhar*; Greek *mimnesko*), knowing that God always remembers the poor, the orphans, the widows, the strangers—those who are marginalized and unjustly treated (Luke 1:55–56; 1 Sam 1:11).

Both Hannah and Mary spoke on behalf of all the Marys of the Bible, and expressed the faith that the God of the Bible always remembers. They knew that God remembered Noah the Just at his deepest time of despair (Gen 8:1); they knew that God always remembers his covenants (Gen 9:15–16); they knew that God has always remembered women who have been in despair (Gen 30:22); they knew that God has heard the cries of the enslaved people in Egypt, and remembered his covenant (Exod 2:24; 6:5).

This God who remembers will never forget all the Marys and the Hannahs of the world.

It becomes clear the Marys and the Hannahs of the world have a deep faith in the God of the Bible. They see all the injustices in the world against the weak and the marginalized. However, in a profound attitude of defiance, they look up to God, and know that he is salvation, *Yeshua*. Therefore, they constantly rejoice and exult. This can be so infuriating to those people who seek to do injustice to them. These women are able to do this, knowing that the God of the Bible will remember them. He will punish those people who do gross injustice to the weak and the vulnerable. These systems of evil and injustice will be brought down. Those people who have endured much hardship and enslavement will experience the *Yeshua*, the salvation, of God.

This was the hope and faith of the Hannahs, Tamars, Rahabs, Bathshebas, and Marys of that time. This will be the hope and faith of the Hannahs, Tamars, Rahabs, Bathshebas, and Marys of today.

MARY AND THE THREAT TO THE LIFE OF HER NEWBORN SON

The second chapter of Matthew brings us a global event. The magi from the East come to worship this King of the Jews (Matt 2:1). A couple of things are important to note: The magi were a group of people who came from the aboriginal people groups. They were against the emperors who enslaved the people groups they conquered. In many senses, they were countercultural prophets from the lower classes. These magi from the East came to Jerusalem, saying, "Where is he who has been born king of the Jews? For we have seen his star in the East, and have come to worship him" (Matt 2:1). In the previous verse, Herod the Great is introduced as the king, but he was a puppet king placed over the conquered people, the Jews. The magi were looking for a king who emerged from the conquered people.

It is worth noting that this was the question which was asked of Jesus at his trial by Pilate. "Are you the king of the Jews?" And Jesus said, "You say so" (Matt 27:11). This was precisely the sign which was put on the cross when Jesus was crucified. "This is Jesus (*Yeshua*), the King of the Jews" (Matt 27:37). Herod the Great tried to kill him in the horrible genocide of baby boys of the *'am ha-aretz*, the low-class people groups, but he did not succeed in doing so because Joseph, Mary, and the baby Yeshua fled to Egypt.

Herod and all Jerusalem, the ruling classes of society—the Herodians, the Pharisees, and the Sadducees—were troubled (Greek *tarrasso*). This is precisely the attitude of the Egyptian pharaoh toward the children of Israel (Exod 14:24; Deut 2:25). Herod ordered a group of neglected thinkers to find out about this event, and sure enough, they acknowledge the words of the prophet Micah, "'But you, Bethlehem, in the land of Judah, are by no means least among the rulers of Judah; for out of you will come a ruler who will shepherd my people Israel'" (Matt 2:6; Mic 5:2 NIV). This prophecy of Micah was earlier affirmed in a beautiful messianic song sung by the aging Jacob, "The scepter will not depart from Judah, nor the ruler's staff from between his feet, until he to whom it belongs shall come (the Messiah King), and the obedience of the nations shall be his" (Gen 49:10 NIV). The same prophecy is uttered by Balaam, the gentile prophet, "I see him, but not now; I behold him, but not near. A star will come out of Jacob; a scepter will rise out of Israel" (Num 24:17 NIV).

Mary has just gone through so much, having delivered a child among the sacrificial lambs in Bethlehem. Now she witnesses her child being worshipped by these legendary countercultural prophets, the magi. The Greek word *proskuneo* is always used of the worship of God in the LXX, the Greek translation of the Hebrew Bible (Gen 18:2; 19:1; 24:26, 48; and so on). Of course this, declaration by an international delegation of countercultural prophets, the magi, necessitated that Mary and Joseph must flee to Egypt.

Why Egypt? This was the place where their ancestors were enslaved and raped, where the King of Egypt, the divine ruler of Egypt, had committed genocide. Why were Mary and Joseph asked to go to this place? The answer is found in the next verse. It is a quote from another prophet, Hosea:

> When Israel was a child, I loved him, and out of Egypt I called my son. But the more they were called, the more they went away from me. They sacrificed to the Baals and they burned incense to images. (Hos 11:1–2 NIV)

Israel, the whole nation, is called "my son" (*liBeni*). They are like Isaac, whom Abraham took to sacrifice (Gen 22:7–8). Moses was asked to tell pharaoh, "Israel is my firstborn son." (Exod 4:22–23). Unfortunately, instead of being the firstborn son, they did horrible things to their own people, and sacrificed "their sons and daughters" to Baals and Molech (Jer 32:35). Now, in an act of faith, when Mary takes her newborn son to Egypt, it is as if she is reversing history. This promised one will begin history anew. He will reverse all the years of injustice and evil against the poor, the orphans, the widows, and the strangers. So, she takes her child to Egypt.

She goes into the unknown, not knowing what will happen in Egypt. A regular piece of advice to a mother is to stick with the known. Do not step into the unknown. But, against all good advice, she takes her child to Egypt, the place of slavery. Back in Bethlehem and all of Judea, Herod ordered the little boys (Greek *paidas*) of the poor villages to be sacrificed. This was a very common practice among the Romans, as was true in Egyptian religions.[37] Sadly, Herod decided to follow this horrible practice.

The narrative goes on to mourn the fact that this horrible act, which was practiced by the kings of Israel and Judah, was carried with vengeance by the conquering kings, as well. Jeremiah the prophet mourns this horrible

37. Much work has been done to describe this awful practice, including Bremmer, *Strange World of Human Sacrifice,* and Schultz, "Romans and Ritual Murder," 516–41.

situation with the words: "A voice is heard in Ramah, weeping and great mourning, Rachel weeping for her children and refusing to be comforted, because they are no more" (Matt 2:18 NIV). Unfortunately, this is the bitter cry of mothers throughout history—during the time in Egypt, during the rule of the kings of Israel and Judah, and now during the time of the birth of Jesus. Rachel and Marys—all mothers—have wept throughout history for the senseless killings and ritual killings of boys and girls.

Even this evil, Jesus seeks to address.

MARY AND JESUS' BAR MITZVAH

One of the hardest and yet most joyous occasions for any mother is to see her son become a man. In Jewish culture, this is when the young lad becomes a *Bar Mitzvah*. During this time in history, Mary is just thankful that her boy was not killed by the cruel ritual sacrifice that Herod carried out. She is also thankful that her boy was not taken into sexual slavery by the Roman soldiers.

Luke 2:41–52 tells the narrative of Jesus' Bar Mitzvah. According to ancient Jewish sources, twelve to thirteen was the age when a Jewish boy became a Bar Mitzvah, i.e., he reached the age of adult accountability.[38] Why did they go during the time of Passover? Scholars vary in their response to this question. Some are of the opinion that Jesus was actually born during the time of Passover. Others are of the opinion that Jesus was conceived during the time of Passover, and was therefore born in December.[39] If Jesus was born during the time of Passover, it is significant that he should be called the Passover lamb, and that he should be born in Bethlehem, in a place where Passover lambs were kept, and that he finally died as the Passover lamb during the time of Passover. It is also significant that the mission of his life be related to Passover.

In this narrative, Jesus, after his Bar Mitzvah, is left behind at the temple. His parents search for him for three days. This is an excruciating time for parents, and especially Mary. She has just see him grow up into a Bar Mitzvah, and now he is nowhere to be seen. Finally, after five days (three days in Jerusalem), she finds him, "in the temple courts, sitting among the teachers, listening to them and asking them questions. Everyone who heard him was amazed at his understanding and his answers" (Luke 2:46–47

---

38. Nid. 5:6; Meg. 4:6; Abot 5:21

39. Schmidt, "Calculating December 25 as the Birth," 542–63.

NIV). Mary was also astonished, and said, "Son, why have you treated us like this? Your father and I have been anxiously searching for you" (Luke 2:48 NIV). To this Jesus responded, "Why were you searching for me . . . Didn't you know I had to be in my Father's house" (Luke 2:49 NIV)? Mary had to come to terms with the fact that she may be his mother, but his primary parent was his Father, YHWH. For Mary, the Bitter One, this would have been a very hard experience. It was something she knew from the time he was conceived, and yet when reality hit, it was hard.

This would be the nature of the relationship between Mary and Jesus. She would always have to remind herself that Jesus' primary goal was to be about the business of his real father (*Abba*). He fulfilled the messianic prophecy of Psalm 69:9, "Zeal for your (the Father's) house will consume me." Any injustice done in the Father's house consumed Jesus, and he castigated those who did unjust things in his Father's house (John 2:17).

When Jesus was thirty years old, he went into the synagogue in his home town of Nazareth and read what might well have been his Bar Mitzvah text: Isaiah 61. It may be noted that the rabbis of the time of the Mishnah and later times removed readings from the Prophets, like Isaiah 61, which are quoted in the New Testament, and make special reference to Jesus. These texts are not read, even today, in the synagogue. However, the Dead Sea Scrolls and other archeological digs have unearthed ancient Jewish reading cycles, which give us lectionary readings from the Prophets. One such cycle is the Palestinian Triennial Cycle. In this, the Torah is read over a period of three years, and is divided into some 154 *sedarim*, or reading sections. In this, at crucial junctures we encounter the texts used in the New Testament. Isaiah 61 is read on quite a few occasions.[40]

In this central text to his mission, Jesus reads:

> "The Spirit of the Lord is on me, because he has anointed me to proclaim good news to the poor. He has sent me to proclaim freedom for the prisoners and recovery of sight for the blind, to set the oppressed free, to proclaim the year of the Lord's favor." (Luke 4:18–19 NIV)

This is the text which Jesus probably read when he became a Bar Mitzvah. This was the text he read when he went into the synagogue as a thirty-year-old. This was his mission statement. It was to bring justice to the poor, the prisoners, the blind, the oppressed, and so on. This is what Jesus

---

40. Perrot, "Reading of the Bible," 137–59.

was discussing with the leaders at the temple when he was twelve years old. This was the business of the Father (*Abba*), and he makes this clear to Mary, his dear mother.

Now many years after that he says, "Today, this scripture is fulfilled in your hearing" (Luke 4:21).

MARY AND THE WEDDING IN CANA OF GALILEE

Another Mary and Jesus encounter happened at a wedding ceremony in Cana of Galilee. It would have been the wedding ceremony of common people, *'am ha-aretz*. At this ceremony, the wine ran out. Mary came to Jesus and said, "They do not have any wine." Jesus says to her, "Woman, my hour has not yet come" (John 2:4).

In the Old Testament, the *hora*, the hour, is always connected with a miraculous breaking through into history of God, as in the miraculous birth of Isaac (Gen 18:10, 14); it is related to the hour when God sends miraculous plagues on the Egyptians, and therefore for all time the people had to remember this "hour" through the Passover (Exod 13:10; Num 9:2, and so on). In the Gospel of John, the word "hour" (*hora*) is used to refer to the death of Jesus on the cross (John 7:30; 8:20; 12:23; 13:1; 17:1, and so on) The hour (*hora*) was historically the time when God breaks through into time and history. He broke through into history specifically in the Passover event, where the Passover lamb was sacrificed, and the blood was sprinkled on the door posts (Exod 12:7, 22, 23). The question is: What was the point of "the wine" and how is it related to "the hour?"

Wine is a crucial symbol in Jewish weddings. All the blessings, and especially the crucial blessing which pronounces the couple as man and wife, are preceded by the drinking of wine: the couple drinks, the rabbi drinks, and all the people drink. Without this, the crucial marriage blessings cannot be recited. In light of this, when the wine ran out, a poor family would not have been able to afford more wine. Jesus did not have to turn the water into wine just so that more people can get drunk; he had to turn the water into wine because without that the marriage ceremony could not go on.

The Jewish Passover ceremony and the Jewish wedding ceremony have many parallels. One of the parallels has to do with the cups of wine, over which blessings are recited. There are four cups:

First, the cup of sanctification. In the Passover, the participant sets oneself apart as holy to partake of this divine feast. In the wedding ceremony, which is preceded by the baptism (*mikveh*), the couple set themselves apart, and purify their whole being for each other.

Second, the cup of judgments. In the Passover, the participants remember the judgments which God brought upon the gods of the Egyptians in the ten plagues. In the wedding ceremony, the couple vow to keep themselves for each other. They promise to not let the loose Egyptian, Sumerian, etc. view of marriage become their perspective on marriage, otherwise they will face the consequences of unfaithfulness.

Third, the cup of redemption. In the Passover, the participant says the blessing that this is the blood of the lamb, the Passover sacrifice. In the wedding, the couple covenant to stay faithful to each other, because the wedding lamb was sacrificed for their oneness.

And finally, the cup of praise. In the Passover, the participant rejoices in the future coming of the Messiah, the bridegroom, who will be married eternally to the bride, Israel. In the wedding ceremony, the bride and the groom partake of this cup, recognizing that their marriage is a picture of the relationship between God and Israel.

In the New Testament, this picture of marriage is taken very seriously. In response to the question regarding divorce, Jesus quoted from Genesis 2:24, "Therefore, a man shall leave his father and mother and cleave to his wife and the two shall become one" (Matt 19:5). Each of the cups of wine represented different stages of becoming one (Hebrew *Echad;* Greek, *mian*), just like God is One (Deut 6:4).

In this narrative of the wedding at Cana, *Yeshua* shows Mary the essential nature of his work. Just like the couple mystically become One through the blessings of the wine, so through the cup of suffering which he takes at the "hour" of his suffering, humanity is bound into oneness with God.

Mary, the Bitter One, knew that the oneness ceremony of marriage was the existential answer to the problem of evil in the world. A young man and a young woman were becoming one. They were snatched out of the hands of human evil, as seen in the rape of virgin boys and girls by Roman soldiers. This oneness was a picture of the oneness of God. So, when Mary went to Jesus and said, "They have no wine," she was asking for this oneness miracle to take place in their lives. Jesus turned the water into wine. In doing so, he showed that he was God, and that through him what mystical oneness takes place between the man and the woman was the biblical solution to evil.

9

Mary Magdalene and the #MeToo Movement

The Gospel of Luke gives the account of certain women who worked with Jesus alongside his twelve disciples:

> After this, Jesus traveled about from one town and village to another, proclaiming the good news of the kingdom of God. The Twelve were with him, and some women who had been cured of evil spirits and diseases: Mary (called Magdalene) from whom seven demons had come out; Joanna the wife of Chuza, the manager of Herod's household; Susanna; and many others. These women were helping to support them out of their own means. While a large crowd was gathering and people were coming to Jesus from town after town. (Luke 8:1–4 NIV)

This narrative makes it clear that the women were faithful supporters of the ministry of Jesus the Messiah. These were women who would have, no doubt, been ostracized by the regular people. They were cured of "evil spirits and diseases."

I have done much work in different parts of the world. However, especially in African countries and in India, I have found many women who are possessed by spiritual forces. A minority of people suffering from this affliction are men, while the majority are women. It seems like physical, emotional, and mental subjugation to human powers makes them more vulnerable to spiritual powers. The sexually oriented rituals that they are forced to participate in makes them more vulnerable to spiritual forces.

This was true during Jesus' days as well. Jesus delivered them from subjection to spiritual forces, as well as mental and physical ailments.

Recent developments in women's mental health—especially in places like India, Peru, South Africa, among other countries—has focused on both of these aspects: mental health on the one hand, and spiritual and psychological health on the other.

The healing of the people possessed by evil spirits and diseases was the main sign of the divine Messiah. A few verses before this text, John had sent his disciples to Jesus and asked him, "Are you he who is to come, or shall we look for another" (Luke 7:18)? When these emissaries came to Jesus, "At that very time Jesus cured many who had diseases, sicknesses and evil spirits, and gave sight to many who were blind. And he answered them, 'Go and tell John what you have seen and heard'" (Luke 7:21–22). The signs of the Messiah included people being healed from evil spirits and diseases.

The women mentioned in this text range all the way from the women of very poor villages, to women who held a higher status in life. Mary, the Bitter One, who is also called Magdalene, in all probability came from a poor family. Joanna's husband was a court official in King Herod's court and probably belonged to the party of the Sadducees. Susanna also came from a wealthy family. So possession by evil forces and mental health issues was not limited to the poor.

These women were "healed of evil spirits and weaknesses" (Greek *hai eisan tetherapeumenai apo pneumaton poneron kai astheinemon*). The Greek text makes it clear that the healing from possession of evil spirits and physical diseases were intrinsically linked together. There is a deep and intrinsic link between the spiritual, mental, emotional, and the physical person. One cannot separate different aspects of the person. When a person goes into a state of depression, it is because of external forms of injustices and persecution, and this person, usually a woman, is subject to "evil spirits."

The Old Testament is replete with the unjust and destructive outcomes of the evil spirits. Here are a few examples: All the evil things which Saul did were attributed to the "evil spirit" (*Ruach ra'a*) (1 Sam 16:14, 15, 16, 23; 19:9). The prophets attribute the evil acts of injustice and violence against the poor, widows, orphans, strangers—all the weak and the vulnerable, as actions done because they are possessed by the "evil spirit," (*ra'a ruach*, Hos 11:2). All forms of violence and bloodshed between people groups and nations are attributed to the "evil spirits" (Judg 9:22–25). The evil spirit brings about jealousy and strife between people. Evil spirits families (Num 5:14,

30; 11:29). The evil spirits are also called "*ruach sheqer.*" These are the spirits of gods which are deceptive, injurious, enticing, treacherous, lying, and so on (1 Kgs 22:22–23; Ps 33:17). These spirits bring the poor and the weak into utter ruin (Isa 32:7; 59:3, 13; Jer 3:23). These evil spirits take women into false religious sexual orgies, which take them further into being bound by the world of the spirits. The intertestamental Wisdom of Solomon expresses these awful religious practices:

> For while they practice either child sacrifices or occult mysteries, or frenzied carousing in exotic rites, they no longer respect either lives or purity of marriage; but they either waylay and kill each other, or aggrieve each other by adultery. And all is confusion—blood and murder, theft and guile, corruption, faithlessness, turmoil, perjury, disturbance of good people, neglect of gratitude, besmirching of souls, unnatural lust, disorder in marriage, adultery and shamelessness. (Wis 14:23–26)

Another intertestamental book describes the consequence of these evil spirits thus:

> The gentiles filled the temple with debauchery and revelry; they amused themselves with prostitutes and had intercourse with women even in the sacred courts. They also brought forbidden things into the temple. (2 Macc 6:4)

Jesus and the apostles address the repercussions of this complex injustice against poor women and men. The religions of the Greeks and the Romans had complex ramifications on the lives of the poor, and Jesus and the apostles address this core issue. Evil spirits were at the root of much evil in society, and so Jesus and the apostles address this core problem squarely.

In the beatitudes, Jesus pronounces the Ten Blesseds (Greek *Makarioi*), which parallel the Ten Commandments. The very first Blessed is, "Blessed are the poor in spirit (Greek *ptochoi pneumatic*) for theirs is the kingdom of heaven" (Matt 5:3). This Blessed is written in Luke as "Blessed are you poor, for yours is the kingdom of God" (Luke 6:20). Two observations may be made here: One, the parallel to this "Blessed" is the first commandment which prohibits the worship of gods. These gods are always made in the image of high-class people like kings and rulers, and therefore are meant to subjugate the poor people and captives into slavery. Therefore, the first of the Ten Commandments prohibits polytheism. And two, we may note that the Gospel of Matthew calls it the "poverty in spirit." This is the deep spiritual, emotional, mental, and psychological evil that is done to the poor and the weak as a result of the religions of divine rulers. The Gospel of Luke focuses on the physical, social, and economic aspects of poverty. It should be noted that both sets of aspects are intrinsically related. Spiritual, religious, and polytheistic injustices always lead to social, economic, and physical poverty. These are the deep evils that the gospel of Jesus seeks to address.

In light of this, the Gospels always stress Jesus' power over the evil spirits and demons. He delivered those poor women who were "possessed by the demons (Greek *daimonizomai*), and he cast out the spirits with his word (Greek *Logos*) and healed (Greek *therapeuo*) those who were in the grip of evil (Greek *kakos*)" (Matt 8:16). This is what Jesus did for Mary Magdalene (Luke 7:21; 8:2). It is clear from a whole range of texts in the Gospels that Jesus viewed evil spirit possession as the primary cause of physical, social, and economic maladies. These led to further injustices, and evils being levied upon poor people. Therefore, he also gave his disciples the authority to cast out "evil, foul, or lewd spirits" (Greek *pneuma akathartos*) (Matt 10:1).

Mark 9:14–29 tells the story of a boy (Greek *paidos*), a child who was vulnerable to the physical and spiritual atrocities of the Romans. In his case, the *pneuma akathartos*, the "evil, foul, or lewd spirits" is also called the "dumb spirit" (Greek *alalos*). Sadly, this is what the poor, the widows, the orphans, and the strangers were considered to be: *alalos*, or dumb. In this narrative, the oppressive spirit caused the boy to go into violent seizures, "whenever it seizes him, it throws him down, and he foams and grinds his teeth and becomes rigid" (Mark 9:18).

This is a scary scene. I have seen this occur several times during my travels to African countries and India. The low-class/caste people have the reputation of being lewd and foul, at the same time they are considered dumb. The gods they are forced to worship possess them and it results in these kinds of physical, mental, and emotional symptoms. In this narrative, the low-class father pleads with Jesus, "'It has often thrown him into fire or water to kill him. But if you can do anything, take pity on us and help us'" (Mark 9:22). Seeing the amazing faith of this commoner father, Jesus rebuked the impure spirit.

> "You deaf and mute spirit," he said, "I command you, come out of him and never enter him again." The spirit shrieked, convulsed him violently and came out. The boy looked so much like a corpse

that many said, "He's dead." But Jesus took him by the hand and lifted him to his feet, and he stood up. (Mar 9:25–27 NIV)

This completely changed the life of the low-class father and son.

In Hebrew, the word *alam* is used of the Messiah in the famous Suffering Messiah text, "He was oppressed and he was afflicted, yet he opened not his mouth, like a lamb that is led to the slaughter, and like a sheep that before its shearers is mute (*alam*), so he opened not his mouth" (Isa 53:7). Similarly, the messianic Psalm of Lament cries out, "I was mute and silent. I held my peace to no avail, and my distress grew worse" (Ps 39:2).

The weak and the oppressed are always considered dumb by oppressive people. The assumption of dumbness enables the oppressor to be more oppressive of the weak. This dumbness many times is a kind of spiritual oppression, and people need deliverance from this spiritual oppression, just like this *paidos*, this slave boy.

The consequences of subjection to the evil spirits caused women and the poor to go into a state of social, physical, emotional, economic, and intellectual "weakness," (Greek *asthenia*). This was the status of the woman in Luke 13:10–17. The NIV translates this as a "woman crippled by a spirit" (Luke 13:11). However, English translations miss the gravity of the Greek text. Jesus proclaims powerfully, "You are freed from your weakness (*asthenia*)" (Luke 13:12). This salvation was not merely a physical healing. It was also an emotional, psychological, social, mental, and economic freedom. No wonder the powers that be were not happy with this deliverance. They wanted people like this woman to continue to be in a state of *asthenia*, of weakness and vulnerability, because it served the interests of the powers that be. When Jesus said, "You are freed from your *asthenia*," he was fulfilling the words of Isaiah, "He took on our *asthenia*" (Matt 8:17; Isa 53:4).

When studying ancient Near Eastern societies and religions, it becomes clear that there is a deep spiritual origin to social, economic, etc., maladies and evil. The Bible seeks to counter this. This is the Spirit that creates beauty and order out of chaos (Gen 1:2); that seeks to meet human beings right in the midst of awful despair (Gen 3:8); that remembers human beings when they do not know how things will turn out (Gen 8:1); which seeks to restore the broken spirits of slaves (Gen 6:9), and takes them out of the grip of evil spirits (Exod 15:8, 10); that gives wisdom and creativity to human beings (Exod 35:31); that enables prophets and leaders to discern the future (Num 11:25); that provides food for the hungry (Num 11:31);

that made leaders out of common human beings like Joshua and Moses (Deut 34:9); that gave common and weak human beings the authority to become judges (Judg 3:10; 6:4; and so on); that empowered prophets like Elijah and Elisha (1 Kgs 18:12; 2 Kgs 2:9); that caused David to repent of his evil (Ps 51:10, 11); which will be upon the Messiah, according to the prophets (Is 11:2; 42:1; 61:1; and so on).

In the New Testament, Jesus the Messiah is born of the Holy Spirit (Greek *Pneumatos Hagiou*) (Matt 1:18, 20); the Holy Spirit was the first to declare the divinity of Jesus (Matt 3:16); and Jesus was constantly led by the Spirit (Matt 4:1). It is by the Spirit that Jesus proclaims justice to the gentiles (Greek *ethnos*), the ones who have experienced the evil impact of evil spirits the most (Matt 12:18, 28). In light of this, very early on in Jesus' ministry, the Holy Spirit is promised to his followers (Mark 1:8).

It is clear that the Good Spirit and the evil spirits are diametrically opposed to each other. A crucial dimension of the gospel of Jesus the Messiah addresses this core concern. It says that individuals and society can be delivered from oppressive and evil spirits, and instead, human beings who have been oppressed can be filled with the Holy Spirit. This would recreate them into new human beings.

Sadly, some, like Mary Magdalene, are oppressed sevenfold. Their demonic oppression is not easy to overcome. Jesus did that with his powerful *Logos*, or word. This practice of casting out evil spirits was practiced by the early church. One instance is found in Acts 16:

> Once when we (Paul along with other women leaders) were going to the place of prayer, we were met by a female slave (Greek *paidiske*) who had a spirit of divination (Greek *pneuma puthon*). She earned a great deal of money for her owners by divination (Greek *manteuomai*). She followed Paul and the rest of us, shouting, "These men are servants of the Most High God, who are telling you the way to be saved." She kept this up for many days. Finally, Paul became so annoyed that he turned around and said to the spirit, "In the name of Jesus Christ I command you to come out of her!" At that moment, the spirit left her. (Acts 16:16–18 NIV)

Greek and Roman religions made much unjust use of *paidiske* and *paidos*, girls and boys who were enslaved by high-class people. They were forced to worship sexually oriented gods, and in the process they were possessed by the spirits of these gods and goddesses. The owners of these sexual slaves, *paidiske and paidos*, would use them however they desired.[41]

Are the phenomena of evil spirits and sexual slavery, along with its complex ramifications, prevalent today? A quick survey of newspapers reporting from different parts of the world—Ukraine, France, Germany, USA, South Africa, Kenya, India, Bangladesh, Pakistan, really, all over the world—reveals that this phenomenon is alive and well. Today it is called human trafficking or sex trafficking. There are a number of organizations which are, thankfully, rescuing and restoring trafficked women, girls, and boys.[42] However, according to my research, none of these organizations are dealing with the roots and basis of this evil (i.e., evil spirits). Unless these organizations consider sex trafficking to be more than an economic and social problem, the solutions will be inadequate at best.

41. Masterson et al., *Sex in Antiquity*. This crucial volume has a number of articles which deal with this awful phenomenon in the religions of the ancient Near East, including in Greek and Roman religions.

42. To name a few: Anti-slavery International; the A21 campaign in Cambodia; Coalition Against Trafficking in Women; Free the Slaves; International Justice Mission; Maiti Nepal; the Not for Sale Campaign; Rahab Ministries in Costa Rica and Thailand; Stop the Traffick; and Women at Risk.

10

Mary of Bethany and the #MeToo Movement

John 12 narrates a poignant incident at the house of Mary, Martha, and Lazarus. In John 11, Jesus raises Lazarus from the dead, as a result of which the Pharisees, seeing their political power diminish, seek to kill Jesus. Sometime after that, "six days before Passover," Jesus comes to Bethany to visit his very close friends, and Mary, the Bitter One, was one of them.

This endeared family served a Passover dinner. *Anakeimai*, to recline, is the Greek word used in the Gospels to describe the Passover dinner (Matt 9:10; 22:10, 11; 26:7; Mark 6:26; 14:18; Luke 22:27; John 6:11, 12:2; 13:23, 26). This Passover dinner is designed to be a remembrance of salvation of the slaves from Egypt. The basic theme of the Passover meal is that the Lord of the Bible always sees, hears, knows, and comes down to deliver the afflicted and enslaved people (Exod 3:7–8). These themes are underlined in these Gospel passages, and each of them have to do with Mary, the Bitter One.

In John 12, Mary, the Bitter One, takes "about a pint of pure nard, an expensive perfume; she poured it on Jesus' feet and wiped his feet with her hair. And the house was filled with the fragrance of the perfume" (John 12:3 NIV). Was this action of Mary described at another time? The Greek words seem to suggest so. Here are three passages which need to be noted:

Matthew 26:6–13

While Jesus was in Bethany in the home of Simon the Leper, a woman came to him with an alabaster jar of very expensive perfume, which she poured on his head as he was reclining at the table. When the disciples saw this, they were indignant. "Why this waste?" they asked. "This perfume could have been sold at a high price and the money given to the poor." Aware of this, Jesus said to them, "Why are you bothering this woman? She has done a beautiful thing to me. The poor you will always have with you, but you will not always have me. When she poured this perfume on my body, she did it to prepare me for burial. Truly I tell you, wherever this gospel is preached throughout the world, what she has done will also be told, in memory of her." (Matt 26:6–13 NIV)

Mark 14:3–10

While he was in Bethany, reclining at the table in the home of Simon the Leper, a woman came with an alabaster jar of very expensive perfume, made of pure nard. She broke the jar and poured the perfume on his head. Some of those present were saying indignantly to one another, "Why this waste of perfume? It could have been sold for more than a year's wages and the money given to the poor." And they rebuked her harshly. "Leave her alone," said Jesus. "Why are you bothering her? She has done a beautiful thing to me. The poor you will always have with you, and you can help them any time you want. But you will not always have me. She did what she could. She poured perfume on my body beforehand to prepare for my burial. Truly I tell you, wherever the gospel is preached throughout the world, what she has done will also be told, in memory of her." Then Judas Iscariot, one of the Twelve, went to the chief priests to betray Jesus to them. (Mar 14:3–10 NIV)

Luke 7:36—8:2

When one of the Pharisees invited Jesus to have dinner with him, he went to the Pharisee's house and reclined at the table. A woman in that town who lived a sinful life learned that Jesus was eating at the Pharisee's house, so she came there with an alabaster jar of perfume. As she stood behind him at his feet weeping, she began to wet his feet with her tears. Then she wiped them with her hair, kissed them and poured perfume on them. When the Pharisee who had invited him saw this, he said to himself, "If this man were a prophet, he would know who is touching him and what kind of woman she is—that she is a sinner." Jesus answered him, "Simon, I have something to tell you." "Tell me, teacher," he said. "Two people owed money to a certain moneylender. One owed him five hundred denarii, and the other fifty. Neither of them had the money to pay him back, so he forgave the debts of both. Now which of them will love him more?" Simon replied, "I suppose the one who had the bigger debt forgiven." "You have judged correctly," Jesus said. Then he turned toward the woman and said to Simon, "Do you see this woman? I came into your house. You did not give me any water for my feet, but she wet my feet with her tears and wiped them with her hair. You did not give me a kiss, but this woman, from the time I entered, has not stopped kissing my feet. You did not put oil on my head, but she has poured perfume on my feet. Therefore, I tell you, her many sins have been forgiven— as her great love has shown. But whoever has been forgiven little loves little." Then Jesus said to her, "Your sins are forgiven." After this, Jesus traveled about from one town and village to another, proclaiming the good news of the kingdom of God. The Twelve were with him, and also some women who had been cured of evil spirits and diseases. (Luke 7:36–8:2 NIV)

John 12: 1–8

Six days before the Passover, Jesus came to Bethany, where Lazarus lived, whom Jesus had raised from the dead. Here a dinner was given in Jesus' honor. Martha served, while Lazarus was among those reclining at the table with him. Then Mary took about a pint of pure nard, an expensive perfume; she poured it on Jesus' feet and wiped his feet with her hair. And the house was filled with the fragrance of the perfume. But one of his disciples, Judas Iscariot, who was later to betray him, objected, "Why wasn't this perfume sold and the money given to the poor? It was worth a year's wages." He did not say this because he cared about the poor but because he was a thief; as keeper of the money bag, he used to help himself to what was put into it. "Leave her alone," Jesus replied. "It was in- tended that she should save this perfume for the day of my burial.

You will always have the poor among you, but you will not always have me." (John 12:1–8 NIV)

It is useful to compare the four Gospel narratives:

1. Matthew, Mark, and John mention that this incident takes place in Bethany. Luke does not mention a place.

2. John mentions the name Mary. Matthew, Mark, and Luke do not mention the name; they simply say, "a woman."

3. All four Gospels mention that this was the time of Passover. Matthew and Luke use the word "reclined"; Mark uses "Feast of Unleavened Bread"; and John uses "Passover."

4. Mark and Matthew mention that this takes place at the house of Simon the Leper; Luke writes, "one of the Pharisees"; John mentions that this is the house of Mary, Martha and Lazarus.

5. All four mention the use of an expensive perfume/ointment.

6. Matthew, Mark, and John mention the opposition of Judas Iscariot regarding the ethics of the use of an expensive ointment for this purpose. "This could have sold for a large sum of money and given to the poor." Of course, in a few days, Judas, the money keeper of the disciples, turned Jesus in to the Pharisees and Sadducees to be crucified.

7. Matthew, Mark, and Luke point out Jesus' response to this, i.e. she had a premonition regarding his death, and therefore anointed his body with oil. In all four narratives, Jesus commends the faith of this woman.

In Luke 10:38–41, this same Mary of Bethany is seen as constantly sitting "at the feet of Jesus." She is absorbing his teaching, and asking him questions. She is depicted as a person who yearns to know her rabbi and Lord. When Martha gets upset about this, because she is having to do all the household chores, Jesus says,

> "Martha, Martha, you are anxious and troubled about many things, but there is only one thing which is most essential, and Mary has chosen that Good inheritance (Greek *Agathe merida*). It will never be taken away (Greek *afaireo*) from her." (Luke 10:41–42)

This taking away of one's inheritance was at the root of poverty, and the enslavement of the poor, the widows, and the marginalized of Bethany. This is what Jesus is stressing in his response. He is in fact saying, "Mary, the Bitter One, will no longer be Bitter. She has chosen the good, just like in Genesis 1."

Most commentaries are divided on who the woman in Matthew, Mark, and Luke narratives is. In the John narrative, it is clear that this is the Mary of Bethany. However, it seems to me that this is an irrelevant issue. All the Marys of the New Testament are subject to the same kind of brutality and sexual slavery. The nameless women of Matthew, Mark, and Luke are also Marys. Mary sat at the feet of Jesus in Luke 10, because she knew how much pain she has gone through. In the "anointing" narratives of the four Gospels, one can picture Mary sitting at the corner, not in the midst of the people, because the regular people would have considered her to be a bad woman. However, Jesus knew why she was in this horrible situation. It was because of the horrible evil that society had brought upon her.

In Luke 7, Jesus says to the Pharisee,

> "Do you see this woman? I came into your house. You did not give me any water for my feet, but she wet my feet with her tears and wiped them with her hair. You did not give me a kiss, but this woman, from the time I entered, has not stopped kissing my feet. You did not put oil on my head, but she has poured perfume on my feet. Therefore, I tell you, her many sins have been forgiven— as her great love has shown. But whoever has been forgiven little loves little." Then Jesus said to her, "Your sins are forgiven." (Luke 7:44–50)

Research in human trafficking and prostitution has shown that 90 percent of the women who are called prostitutes were forcibly raped by traffickers when they were minors 13–16 years old, or even younger in some countries.[43] Some research shows that they are gang raped by the traffickers on the first day. Their identity is completely shattered when they are sexual slaves. This horrible picture must be multiplied many times in order to understand what the Marys of the time of Jesus went through. This was done by the cruel Roman soldiers.

In Luke 7, when Jesus says, "Your sins are forgiven," he is pronouncing healing upon this woman who has experienced so much pain. This is what is emphasized in what follows, "After this, Jesus traveled about from one

---

43. Hunter, "Prostitution Is Cruelty and Abuse," 91–104.

town and village to another, proclaiming the good news of the kingdom of God. The Twelve were with him, and also some women who had been cured of evil spirits and diseases" (Luke 8:1–2 NIV). This woman, Mary, was one of the people who was holistically—spiritually, physically, mentally, emotionally, socially, and economically—healed, and she served Jesus in his ministry.

Was this Mary Magdalene? Was this Mary of Bethany? The text of the Gospels would have made this clear, should it be of particular importance. What is important is that she was a woman. She was Mary, the Bitter One, and Jesus healed her.

11

All the Marys at the Cross, and the #MeToo Movement

Each of the Gospels mention many women at the cross. These were from among the *laos,* `*am ha-aretz*, the lower-class people from the villages and towns. These were not the high-class people like the Pharisees, Sadducees, Herodians, and the like. John is the only disciple who is mentioned as being at the cross in John's Gospel. Luke also records that a great multitude of low-class people and women followed him mourning and lamenting as they went. These sounds, both in Hebrew and in Greek, were commonly heard among the poor people (Luke 8:52). Matthew and Mark mention that there was darkness from noon till early evening. The mention of this detail is intentional. It is as if the whole world is getting back to its pre-creation state (Gen 1:2). Darkness was the penultimate plague, when the LORD delivered the enslaved people from Egypt. The gospel writers seek to underline this, since Jesus is portrayed as the Passover lamb (Matt 27:45; Mark 15:33).

At this time, Jesus sang a psalm of lament. It was Psalm 22. The first words of the psalm are "*'Eloi, Eloi, Lema Sabachthani,'* which means 'My God, My God, why have you forsaken me?'" It was a familiar song sung during Passover, by the exiled and enslaved children of Israel. We can well imagine the women and the low-class *laos* singing this communal Psalm of Lament with Jesus. It expresses the hope of *Yeshua*, or salvation (Ps 22:1). With his mother and the other Marys he cried,

My God, my God, why have you forsaken me?

Why are you so far from saving me, so far from my cries of anguish?

My God, I cry out by day, but you do not answer, by night,

but I find no rest

Yet you are enthroned as the Holy One;

you are the one Israel praises.

In you our ancestors put their trust;

they trusted and you delivered them.

To you they cried out and were saved;

in you they trusted and were not put to shame.

But I am a worm and not a man,

scorned by everyone,

despised by the people.

All who see me mock me;

they hurl insults, shaking their heads.

"He trusts in the LORD," they say, "let the LORD rescue him.

Let him deliver him, since he delights in him."

Yet you brought me out of the womb;

you made me trust in you, even at my mother's breast.

From birth, I was cast on you;

from my mother's womb, you have been my God.

Do not be far from me, for trouble is near and there is no one to
help.

Many bulls surround me; strong bulls of Bashan encircle me.

Roaring lions that tear their prey open their mouths wide against
me.

I am poured out like water, and all my bones are out of joint.

My heart has turned to wax; it has melted within me.

My mouth is dried up like a potsherd,

and my tongue sticks to the roof of my mouth; you lay me in the
dust of death.

Dogs surround me, a pack of villains encircles me; they pierce my
hands and my feet.

All my bones are on display; people stare and gloat over me.

They divide my clothes among them and cast lots for my garment.

But you, LORD, do not be far from me.

You are my strength; come quickly to help me.

Deliver me from the sword, my precious life from the power of
the dogs.

Rescue me from the mouth of the lions; save me from the horns
of the wild oxen.

I will declare your name to my people; in the assembly, I will praise
you.

You who fear the LORD, praise him!
All you descendants of Jacob, honor him! Revere him, all you descendants of Israel!
For he has not despised or scorned the suffering of the afflicted one; he has not hidden his face from him but has listened to his cry for help.
From you comes the theme of my praise in the great assembly; before those who fear you, I will fulfill my vows.
The poor will eat and be satisfied;
those who seek the LORD will praise him—may your hearts live forever!
All the ends of the earth will remember and turn to the LORD,
and all the families of the nations will bow down before him,
for dominion belongs to the LORD and he rules over the nations.
All the rich of the earth will feast and worship;
all who go down to the dust will kneel before him—
those who cannot keep themselves alive.
Posterity will serve him; future generations will be told about the Lord.
They will proclaim his righteousness, declaring to a people yet unborn: He has done it! (Ps 22:1–31)

This psalm is not just a Psalm of Lament, which it is, but like all Psalms of Lament, it always ends in hope that the *Yeshua* of God will finally bring about justice, wholeness, and peace. In many senses, just like the songs of all the Marys in the Bible, this also is a song of revolt, in the face of the most awful form of punishment and evil, ever invented by humanity:

They despised me, but I will reach out to them, and love them. (Ps 22:6)

I knew this was my lot from my mother's womb. (Ps 22:9)

They brought me to the dust of death, but I will rise again. (Ps 22:15)

They pierced my hands and my side, but I will rise again, and these wounds will be healed. (Ps 22:16)

They divided my garments among them, and for my clothing they cast lots. That is indeed what they did to Joseph. Just like Joseph, I will overcome as well. (Ps 22:18)

145

This is the depth of darkness.

"Yet, all the ends of the world, all the families of the nations will worship You" (Ps 22:27). This is the goal of this horrible punishment.

When Jesus, and all the Marys sang this song, it must have been so perplexing to the soldiers, and all the people who crucified him, but the low class hearers knew the vast importance of this song. They had sung this so many times before, in the hope of a Messiah. And now, here he was.

Right after this, the soldiers take a sponge and fill it with *Chametz*, or sour wine (Ps 69:21). In the Hebrew Bible, *Chametz* is a sign of human evil. It is given to women so that religious sexual practices can be perpetrated against them. It is given to low-class servants so that their utter servitude may be bearable, and so that harder labor may be expected of them. Instead of *Chametz*, the people are supposed to be eating only *Matzah* (unleavened bread).

The book of John mentions a very poignant interaction between Jesus, his mother Mary, and John himself. Among his last words, Jesus looked at the sad eyes of his mother, and then he saw John. He said to his mother, "Woman behold your son." And to John he said, "Behold your mother" (John 19:26, 27). Jesus knew that his mother had seen much pain and bitterness in her life. She was soon going to be left son-less. The son-mother relationship throughout history has been considered to be a very intense relationship. Jesus was the one who protected her from all bitterness. Now, he was handing the task over to his closest disciple, John.

It is for this reason that sons were considered to be very important, and are still very important in the East and the West. In some senses this transaction was very similar to the Ruth and Boaz transaction. In that case, Naomi gained a new son, as a result of the *Go'el* relationship. There is much social, psychological, emotional, and mental healing which develops as a result of this provision of a son.

Jesus, the women, the Marys, and John had sung the Psalms of Lament. It was like an amazing worship service, at this dark hour. After this, Jesus knew that his task was accomplished. In the hearing of John, and the women, the Marys, he cried out, "It is finished" (John 19:30).

Mary, the mother of Jesus, would well have known these words. The Gospel of Matthew begins with the words, "The book of the generations of *Yeshua* the Messiah." The book began in Genesis 1:1. An ancient interpretation of the Hebrew Bible is found in the Targum. These are Aramaic translations of the Hebrew Bible. Aramaic was the *lingua franca*, common official language, during the time of Daniel. It was the language of the low-class people, the *laos*, the `am ha-aretz*, during the time of Jesus. One of the Targums, Targum Yerushalmi, translates Genesis 1:1 this way, "In the beginning, the Word of God, the Son of God, with wisdom and understanding created and finished the heavens and the earth." Mary and the poor people knew this prophecy of the messianic hope.

When God created the heavens and the earth, the text says, "God finished." (Gen 2:1, 2). Whenever God breaks through into history, this is recorded by God finishing, for example when God gave Moses the Ten Commandments, "He finished" (Exod 31:18). When Moses completed the task of building all the worship material and the Tabernacle, the text says, "Moses finished" (Exod 40:33). When Moses completed the task of giving them the Torah, the text says, "Moses finished" (Deut 32:45; Exodus 34:33). When the temple was constructed, the same words are used, "he finished" (1 Kgs 7:51; 8:54). This process is seen at several junctures in the Hebrew Bible.

When the New Testament describes the work of Jesus the Messiah, it continues with the same words.

In Matthew 7:28, "Jesus finished the teaching" of the ten Blesseds, which parallel the Ten Commandments, and finished giving his code of ethics. These are the Torah of Jesus.

In Matthew 11:1, Jesus "finished instructing his disciples." These are the prophetic utterances of Jesus.

In Matthew 13:53, "Jesus finished teaching the parables." These are the Psalms and the wisdom literature of Jesus.

In Matthew 19:1, "Jesus finished teaching his disciples" regarding the laws of love and forgiveness.

In Matthew 26:1, "Jesus finished his apocalyptic teaching."

Finally, John records his last words, "It is finished."

What did he finish? The events recorded right after Jesus' first "finished" (Matt 7:28) give us a clear answer to this:

> When evening came, many who were demon-possessed were brought to him, and he drove out the spirits with a word and healed all the sick. This was to fulfill what was spoken through the prophet Isaiah: "He took up our infirmities and bore our diseases." (Matt 8:16–17, Isa 53:4 NIV)

Jesus fulfilled all the prophetic poems of the suffering divine Messiah of the Hebrew Bible. Isaiah 53 is one example:

Who has believed our message
and to whom has the arm of the LORD been revealed?
He grew up before him like a tender shoot,
and like a root out of dry ground.
He had no beauty or majesty to attract us to him,
nothing in his appearance that we should desire him.
He was despised and rejected by mankind,
a man of suffering, and familiar with pain.
Like one from whom people hide their faces he was despised,
and we held him in low esteem.
Surely, he took up our pain and bore our suffering,
yet we considered him punished by God, stricken by him, and afflicted.
But he was pierced for our transgressions,
he was crushed for our iniquities;
the punishment that brought us peace was on him,
and by his wounds we are healed.
We all, like sheep, have gone astray,
each of us has turned to our own way;
and the LORD has laid on him the iniquity of us all.
He was oppressed and afflicted, yet he did not open his mouth;
he was led like a lamb to the slaughter,
and as a sheep before its shearers is silent, so he did not open his mouth.
By oppression and judgment, he was taken away.
Yet who of his generation protested? For he was cut off from the land
   of the living; for the transgression of my people he was punished.
He was assigned a grave with the wicked,
and with the rich in his death,
though he had done no violence, nor was any deceit in his mouth.
Yet it was the LORD's will to crush him and cause him to suffer,
and though the LORD makes his life an offering for sin, he will see
   his offspring and prolong his days,
and the will of the LORD will prosper in his hand.
After he has suffered, he will see the light of life and be satisfied;
by his knowledge my righteous servant will justify many,
and he will bear their iniquities. (Isa 53:1–11 NIV)

The words which are expressed of the passion of the Messiah are all the pains and sorrows of the Marys of the world—the poor, the widows, the strangers. The Hebrew words expressed in this song describe evils with mental, physical, spiritual, and psychological ramifications. These are systemic evils and injustices with social, racial, economic, and spiritual ramifications. When the Marys and #MeToo victims of the world hear Jesus' final words, "It is finished," it takes on a profound and mindboggling significance. It brings about healing beyond comprehension. I have seen this happen in different parts of the world.

Significantly, the prophetic poem in Isaiah 53 does not end with the death of the Messiah:

> He will see the light of life, and by his knowledge my just Servant
> will justify many. (Isa 53:11)

It looks forward to the resurrection.

12

All the Marys at the Resurrection of Jesus the Messiah and the #MeToo Movement

The Gospels of Matthew, Mark, and Luke record,

> The women who had come with Jesus from Galilee followed Joseph and saw the tomb and how his body was laid in it. Then they went home and prepared spices and perfumes. But they rested on the Sabbath in obedience to the commandment. (Luke 23:55–56 NIV).

These were all the Marys.

Then all four Gospels record that it was the Marys who were the first ones to go to the tomb on the first day of the week, while it was still dark. Matthew records,

> After the Sabbath, at dawn on the first day of the week, Mary Magdalene and the other Mary went to look at the tomb. There was a violent earthquake, for an angel of the Lord came down from heaven and, going to the tomb, rolled back the stone and sat on it. His appearance was like lightning, and his clothes were white as snow. The guards were so afraid of him that they shook and became like dead men. The angel said to the women, "Do not be afraid, for I know that you are looking for Jesus, who was crucified. He is not here; he has risen, just as he said. Come and see the place where he lay. Then go quickly and tell his disciples: 'He has risen

from the dead and is going ahead of you into Galilee. There you will see him.' Now I have told you." (Matt 28:1–7 NIV)

Luke records,

While they were wondering about this, suddenly two men in clothes that gleamed like lightning stood beside them. In their fright the women bowed down with their faces to the ground, but the men said to them, "Why do you look for the living among the dead? He is not here; he has risen!" (Luke 24:4–6 NIV)

John records,

Early on the first day of the week, while it was still dark, Mary Magdalene went to the tomb and saw that the stone had been removed from the entrance. So, she came running to Simon Peter and the other disciple, the one Jesus loved, and said, "They have taken the Lord out of the tomb, and we don't know where they have put him!" (John 20:1–2 NIV)

All the Gospels are very clear that it was all the Marys who were the first witnesses to this greatest event in human history—the resurrection of Jesus the Messiah. The Gospels underline the fact that it is the Marys who have endured the most evil and misery, and who were the main witnesses to Jesus' pain and suffering on the cross. It was not the who's who of the religious leadership, be it Jewish or gentile. The Gospels also underline that it was the Marys who were the first to witness the resurrection, not the male disciples.

The Gospel of Mark underscores this with the comment,

"But go, tell his disciples and Peter, 'He is going ahead of you into Galilee. There you will see him, just as he told you.'" Trembling and bewildered, the women went out and fled from the tomb. They said nothing to anyone, because they were afraid. (Mark 16:7–8 NIV)

This is the shorter ending of the Gospel of Mark. The longer ending goes on to record,

When Jesus rose early on the first day of the week, he appeared first to Mary Magdalene, out of whom he had driven seven demons. She went and told those who had been with him and who were mourning and weeping. (Mark 16:9–10 NIV)

The Gospel of Mark may well have ended on the note that these Marys were "afraid," as the most ancient manuscripts of the Gospel of Mark end. No doubt they were afraid. All they had seen throughout their lives was nothing but bitterness and fear. However, it is worth noting that the longer ending seeks to underscore that

> he appeared first to Mary Magdalene, out of whom he had driven seven demons. She went and told those who had been with him and who were mourning and weeping. (Mark 16:9)

These were the demons which had taken control of her through the religious, political, social, and economic systems of the enslavement society of her day. But, they were cast out by Jesus the Messiah, and so she had the courage to go and give them the good news, "He is risen" (Matt 28:7).

The Gospel of John records perhaps the most enduring resurrection picture.

> Now Mary stood outside the tomb crying. As she wept, she bent over to look into the tomb and saw two angels in white, seated where Jesus' body had been, one at the head and the other at the foot. They asked her, "Woman, why are you crying?" "They have taken my Lord away," she said, "and I don't know where they have put him." At this, she turned around and saw Jesus standing there, but she did not realize that it was Jesus.
>
> He asked her, "Woman, why are you crying? Who is it you are looking for?" Thinking he was the gardener, she said, "Sir, if you have carried him away, tell me where you have put him, and I will get him." Jesus said to her, "Mary." She turned toward him and cried out in Aramaic, "Rabboni!" (which means "Teacher"). Jesus said, "Do not hold on to me, for I have not yet ascended to the Father. Go instead to my brothers and tell them, 'I am ascending to my Father and your Father, to my God and your God.'" Mary Magdalene went to the disciples with the news: "I have seen the Lord!" And she told them that he had said these things to her. (John 20:11–18 NIV)

That existential moment was so important for Mary, and all the Marys of the world. Jesus said, "Mary, Oh Bitter One!" And, Mary said, "Rabboni, my Teacher, my Messiah." That was the all-important healing moment. It was the healing moment of Mary Magdalene, "out of whom he had driven seven demons," and for all the Marys of the world, out of whom millions of demons are driven.

Conclusion

The #MeToo movement is a powerful reminder of the abuses faced by women in our society today. In this book, I have tried to show that these abuses are global, and have been global issues throughout the history of humanity. Sadly, ancient religions have been the basis of this abuse, as is true of modern religions and modern secularism. The Hebrew Bible stresses this right at the very beginning of the Genesis 3 narrative of Eve. The New Testament stresses this right at the very beginning in the genealogy of Jesus the Messiah. Both the Hebrew Bible and the New Testament seek to show that this two-part canon of the Christian church is indeed the original #MeToo movement.

In each of the chapters of this book, I have sought to derive solutions of the Bible's #MeToo movement. In the first chapter, I have stressed that Jesus' mother is the primary focus of the biblical #MeToo movement. Her name was Mary, as were so many girls in the land that was controlled by the Romans. The name Mary means bitter. Girls were called "Mary" because the Roman soldiers went around the villages, raping girls and using them as sexual slaves. Rape was a method of war, and the parents knew, sadly, that the lives of their baby girls would be bitter. The biblical answer to this horrible #MeToo crisis is seen in the most crucial verse of Matthew 1, "The virgin will conceive and give birth to a son, and they will call him Immanuel (which means "God with us")" (Matt 1:23 NIV). This is a quote from the prophet Isaiah. It is as if the New Testament is thumbing its nose at the power of Rome, and indeed all the powers of the past, present, and future to say, "Regardless of the abuses you may devise against women, a virgin will still remain." This virgin was Mary. She is shown to be representative of other Marys who were saved from the brutal abuse of the Roman soldiers, and soldiers throughout history. The child that was born was called "Immanuel." This was God himself. Therefore, the virgin birth of Jesus, and the

153

incarnation of God, are the most profound solution of the #MeToo movement of the Bible.

The #MeToo women, then and now, can look to Mary, the mother of Jesus, and the incarnation of God, as signs of hope, healing, and salvation. This is one of the most profound truths of the Bible. It seems like it is for this reason that the virgin birth of Jesus is a central credal statement of the Christian church. It is a deep solution to the cries of the #MeToo women, both then and now.

Another solution that I have stressed in the first chapter is to show the role of the #MeToo men. Unless men actively participate in solving the issues brought forward by the #MeToo movement, the solutions may not have far-reaching effects. When men call out the abuse of abusers, it takes on a more effective solution. It is indeed heartening to see men joining in the modern #MeToo movement. It was reassuring to see thousands of young men join the protests led by female college students in protests across India when "India's Daughter," Jyoti, was brutally raped in December of 2012.

In chapter 2, I have shown how Tamar is a strong woman. When she was abused by the men in her life, she took matters into her own hands and found a solution. As a result of this, her abuser was forced to acknowledge in the presence of other judges, "You are more just than I" (Gen 38:26). This kind of sentence was unthinkable coming from a patriarch at that time in history, yet he was forced to be humiliated in front of the who's who of that time. Tamar was a minority foreigner. Her voice could not have been heard by society, and yet she came up with a very unorthodox solution. Indeed, she turned the very method of abuse into her freedom from abuse, so she is called the most just woman. The biblical #MeToo solution here is very unorthodox. Most conservative societies, then and now, would frown upon the solution practiced by Tamar for her awful predicament. Yet the #MeToo movement called the Bible unashamedly honors Tamar for her strategy to gain victory over her abuse and abuser. Unorthodox methods, it seems clear to me, will be found by the abused women of the #MeToo movement. This should be encouraged by the church, just as it was encouraged by the Bible.

In chapter 3, I have delineated the lessons learned from the Rahab narrative. It seems clear to me that, just like the commission given to the Exodus community, the church needs to take its mission seriously: to go into places throughout the world and find the Rahabs of the world. These are women who are abused by global societies for one reason or another.

They are called by abusive names like "Rahab" or "the broads," so that it makes it easier for abusers to abuse them. Abusive names and vocabulary need to be wiped out from all languages so that abuse will be wiped out.

Rahab was forced to live on the periphery of society, where abuse was frequent. This is common in global society even today. When women can get into the mainstream of society as leaders in academics, business, etc., abuse is less likely to happen. Abuse happens when men are in power over women and there are no other women who can curtail the abuse of this power. This became clear in the recent scandal concerning Dr. Larry Nassar, the head physician of the USA Gymnastic team, and the scores of women and girls he sexually abused. If there was a woman who was in a position of responsibility equal to that of this doctor, abuse of these amazing gymnasts would have been less likely.

In chapter 4, I reflect on the beautiful story of Naomi, Ruth, and Boaz. In keeping with the role of Naomi, it seems so crucial that society in general come up with a plan for more experienced women mentoring younger women, a sister-mentoring-sister plan. Women of experience are in the best place to mentor and nurture younger women. Human trafficking and abuse of younger women happens in places where there is no such system. In the story of Ruth, Naomi assumes this role as she mentors Ruth through the complexities of life in a foreign land, where Ruth was most vulnerable to trafficking and abuse. Naomi mentored Ruth with tools of how to interact with men in a foreign land, with dignity and equality, and how not to put herself in a position of vulnerability.

Similarly, Boaz is shown as a strong ally of the #MeToo movement. He took the lead to make sure that a foreign woman like Ruth would never be put in a place of vulnerability, where she could potentially be abused. It seems like society needs to come up with plans like this, which protect women from being abused by people in power. If only Hollywood had had plans like this in place, the abuse suffered by Hollywood women actors at the hands of men like Harvey Weinstein would have been less likely to happen.

Perhaps the most important lesson from the Ruth story is the principle of the recreation of a new economy and new womanhood, where abuse never happens. There are several principles in the Torah which were grossly neglected by society. However, Boaz dug deep into the meaning and relevance of laws like kinsman redeemership and levirate marriage, and derived #McToo principles from these old and neglected laws. He used them to do two things: one, to recreate a new economy and society, where the abuse of women and the vulnerable never happens; and two, to create a new womanhood, where one is never vulnerable to abuse and trafficking. Ruth was dignified and recreated into a new woman.

These are two principles which are very relevant to global society even today. Abuse happens, even today, because of the economic and social place of vulnerability of women. I saw this in the slum where I was reared. In contrast to this, I have also heard a low caste woman say things like the following after a micro-financing plan helped give her a new outlook: "He has beaten me for the last twenty years. I have my own small business. I can stand on my own two feet. Dare he touch me now." Statements like these are powerful. Because of organizations like HOLD, Congo, and Zimele Wethu, South Africa, I have heard women say similar things. This is what I call the Boaz principle to address the cries of the #MeToo movement.

Laws of countries like India, Kenya, Nigeria, etc., need to be reformed. In the Book of Ruth, Boaz applied the principles of land laws and the marital laws of the Torah well. He did this to address economic and gender issues of injustice. This, I have suggested, is a great example of the biblical #MeToo movement. These laws were very distinct from the laws of the Code of Hammurabi and Egyptian laws. The Torah dignified and recreated new women. There is a need for laws like these in countries where women are the most vulnerable and likely to be abused.

Recently laws have been passed where women in Saudi Arabia are permitted to drive. That is a good start; however, there are several other laws which prevent them from even seeking a driver's license. All this is happening, while the rest of the world looks in the other direction, because these #MeToo women of Saudi Arabia are too distant from the modern Western society.

There is a great and urgent need for global legal reforms, especially in laws related to women and girls. These laws, I suggest, should make it absolutely impossible for women and girls to be vulnerable to abuse and trafficking. The story of Boaz and Ruth makes another #MeToo principle very clear. Ruth is portrayed as an *Eshet Chayil*, a strong woman: a physically, emotionally, mentally, and physically strong woman. When a woman is portrayed with strong words like this then there is no need for patriarchal terms like "protection of women." In the Hebrew Bible, the book of Proverbs ends with the portrayal of an *Eshet Chayil*, in Proverbs 31:10–31. This woman is portrayed as the CEO and CFO of several companies. She is not merely a house-bound wife. This strong poem is then followed by the analysis of the #MeToo message of five books: Song of Songs, Ruth, Ecclesiastes, Lamentations, and Esther. Each of these is a commentary on the principle of *Eshet Chayil* in several contexts. In a follow-up to this book, I plan to expand on the #MeToo principles of this book, in another monograph.

In chapter 5, I delineate the #MeToo principles found in the story of David and Bathsheba. David took advantage of a pretty woman, because that is what kings did during that time, and because Uriah the Hittite and his wife were in a vulnerable place. It seems crucial that laws be written in different countries which do not place the modern Uriahs and Bathshebas in similar situations. People in power always take advantage of low-class and low-caste people under their authority. The #MeToo movement as it relates to media moguls is a case in point. Actors and news reporters have to be able to rise up and do well based on their gifts and talents; however, they should never be in a place where people in power take advantage of their place in society, that causes them to be vulnerable. The Torah prescribed such laws for the Jewish kings. They had to be under the Torah and under the guidance of the prophets. Deuteronomy 17:14–20 describes this prescription. For this reason, David was forced to confront his evil before God and the prophet Nathan.

Film and media moguls should not be in a place where they can take advantage of women or men. They always must know that they are subject to the law. Prophets of society, including the church and journalists, need to always be looking out for the concerns of women who may be in positions of vulnerability, and give them voice. Of course this requires fearlessness on the part of the prophets of our time. This fearlessness comes from the realization that prophets are not merely to subscribe to the norms and ethos of society around them, but rather to a higher power—God himself. This is the voice which the Christian church needs to regain in modern times.

What happens when there is abuse of religious power in the Christian church? The Bible gives a clear answer to this. There is a balance of power between the prophets, priests, and kings. All three offices of power are ultimately subject to God. No one has complete control. Further, each position of authority keeps the other in check, and is ultimately subject to God. Unfortunately, this lack of balance of power, and the the lack of realization that everyone is subject to God, has led to abuse in the church, be it in Roman Catholic, Orthodox, or Protestant churches. This issue must be dealt with urgently for the church to regain its moral place of being a beacon of the biblical #MeToo movement.

In chapter 6, I go back to the Genesis narratives. The creation of Eve is a crucial #MeToo principle. She is the mother of all life. She is created in the image of God, just as much as the man. Most of all, she is not merely a "helper or helper suitable for him," but rather she is an *Ezer Kanegdo,* a godlike leader. This creation text sets the stage for what I consider to be the most important #MeToo principle: it calls for a reset of all images of the woman, through history, and both in the East and the West. If only human beings would take this creation principle seriously, there would be no abuse of women.

Sadly, men in power have used drugs and alcohol to put women in places of vulnerability, and then abuse them. Woefully, this is far too common on college campuses. This has recently gained prominence in the trials of athletes and Hollywood actors. This is nothing new. It has been happening in society from ancient times. The biblical #MeToo answer in Genesis 3 is the covenant of the seed of the woman. It prophesies that the woman and her seed, the Messiah, will eventually destroy this abuse and abusive religions. This is the crux of the gospel. The Messiah, the seed of the woman, has come to destroy all abuse of women at the hands of powerful men.

The #MeToo movement has made it clear that ultimately this problem is a deeper problem. Laws and judgment in courts can address the concerns of the #MeToo movement only at the superficial level. It is only the death of the Messiah on the cross which can radically transform global society so that the abuse of women does not happen. All other responses are thin ones, whereas the cross is the thick biblical response to the issues raised by the #MeToo movement.

The Bible hears and has heard the cries of so many Marys of the world, throughout history: Eve, Hagar, Miriam, the Marys of the Gospels, and yes, the Marys of today. To each one the risen Christ says, "Mary, Mary, Mary, I have indeed seen, over and over again, your affliction throughout history at the hands of your Egyptian lords. I have heard your cries because of your sexual, mental, and psychological enslavement and abuse. I personally and experientially know your sufferings. I have come down to deliver you out of the hand of the Egyptian enslavers, and to bring you up out into a good land, so that you will experience complete salvation and healing." (cf. Exod 3:6–8)

The Marys of the Gospels were the only disciples of Jesus, except for John, who stood with him at the cross, The cross of Jesus is the ultimate biblical answer to the cries of the modern and historical #MeToo movement.

John was the only male disciple of Jesus who stood beside the Marys of the Gospels. It seems clear that he is the only one of the male disciples of Jesus who also heard the cries of the Marys. At the cross, Jesus said to Mary, his mother, keeping in mind Genesis 3, "Woman behold your son." To John he said, "Behold your mother" (John 19:26, 27).

The responsibility entrusted to John is the responsibility of the church. It is to take care of all the Marys of the world, and ensure that further abuse and trafficking of the Marys of society ceases forever.

Having given this last commission, Jesus cried, "It is finished."

Bibliography

Acharya, Arun Kumar. "Trafficking of Women in Mexico and Their Health Risk: Issues and Problems." *Cogitatio* 3.1 (2015) 103–12.

Bhalla, Nita. "Almost 20,000 Women and Children Trafficked in India in 2016." https://www.reuters.com/article/us-india-trafficking/almost-20000-women-and-children-trafficked-in-india-in-2016-idUSKBN16G29G.

Black, Maggie. "Women in Ritual Slavery: Devadasi, Jogini, and Mathamma in Karnataka and Andhra Pradesh, Southern India." *Pakistan Journal of Women's Studies: Alam-E-Niswan* 16.1–2 (n.d.) 179–205.

Bremmer, Jan N., ed. *The Strange World of Human Sacrifice*. Dudley, MA: Peeters, 2006.

Brenner, Athalya. *A Feminist Companion to the Hebrew Bible in the New Testament.* Feminist Companion to the Bible 3. Sheffield, UK: Sheffield Academic Press, 2001.

Bühler, Georg. *The Laws of Manu: Translated, with Extracts from Seven Commentaries.* Vol. 25. The Sacred Books of the East. Oxford: Clarendon, 1886.

Camp, Claudia V., and Carole R. Fontaine, eds. Women, *War, and Metaphor: Language and Society in the Study of the Hebrew Bible*. Semeia 61. Atlanta: Scholars, 1993.

Clines, David J. A. "Job." In *New Bible Commentary: 21st Century Edition*, edited by D. A. Carson and Donald Guthrie, 459–84. Downers Grove, IL: InterVarsity, 1994.

Connor, Alice. *Fierce: Women of the Bible and Their Stories of Violence, Mercy, Bravery, Wisdom, Sex, and Salvation*. Minneapolis: Fortress, 2017.

Daniel, Frank Jack, and Satarupa Bhattacharjya. "Asaram Bapu's View on Delhi Rape Raises Anger, but Shared by Many." *Reuters.* January 9, 2013. https://in.reuters.com/article/india-delhi-gang-rape-asaram-bapu-views/asaram-bapus-view-on-delhi-rape-raises-anger-but-shared-by-many-idINDEE90809L20130109.

Day, John. *God's Conflict with the Dragon and the Sea: Echoes of a Canaanite Myth in the Old Testament*. University of Cambridge Oriental Publications 35. Cambridge: Cambridge University Press, 1985.

"Delhi Gang-Rape Case: PM Manmohan Singh Condoles Girl's Death." *Times of India.* December 29, 2012. https://timesofindia.indiatimes.com/city/delhi/Delhi-gang-rape-case-PM-Manmohan-Singh-condoles-girls-death/articleshow/17804055.cms.

Dhillon, Amrit. "Indian Judge Jails 'God Man' for 20 Years for Rape of Two Women." *The Guardian.* August 28, 2017. https://www.theguardian.com/world/2017/aug/28/indian-court-sentences-god-man-to-10-years-in-prison-gurmeet-ram-rahim-singh.

Eriksson Baaz, Maria. "Why Do Soldiers Rape? Masculinity, Violence, and Sexuality in the Armed Forces in the Congo (DRC)," *International Studies Quarterly* 53.2 (2009) 495–518.

Farley, Melissa, ed. *Prostitution, Trafficking and Traumatic Stress.* 4 vols. *Journal of Trauma Practice* 3. Binghamton, NY: Haworth Maltreatment & Trauma, 2003.

Gaca, Kathy. "Ancient Warfare and the Ravaging Martial Rape of Girls and Women: Evidence from Homeric Epic and Greek Drama." In *Sex in Antiquity: Exploring Gender and Sexuality in the Ancient World,* edited by Mark Masterson, et al., 278–97. New York: Routledge, 2015.

———. "Martial Rape, Pulsating Fear, and the Sexual Maltreatment of Girls (παῖδες), Virgins (παρθένοι), and Women (γυναῖκες)." *The American Journal of Philology* 135.3 (2014) 303–57.

Garcia, Sandra E. "The Woman Who Created #MeToo Long Before Hashtags." *New York Times.* October 20, 2017. https://www.nytimes.com/2017/10/20/us/me-too-movement-tarana-burke.html.

Gordon, Pamela, and Harold C. Washington. "Rape as a Military Metaphor in the Hebrew Bible." In *A Feminist Companion to the Latter Prophets,* edited by Athalya Brenner and Carole R. Fontaine, 308–25. Sheffield, UK: Sheffield Academic Press, 1995.

Grayson, Albert Kirk. *Assyrian Royal Inscriptions, Part 2: From Tiglath-Pileser I to Ashur-Nasir-Apli II.* Wiesbaden, Germany: Otto Harrassowitz, 1976.

Griffith, Ralph T. H., trans. *Hinduism: The Rig Veda.* Vol. 5. Sacred Writings. New York: Book-of-the-Month Club, 1992.

Griffith-Jones, Robin. *Beloved Disciple: The Misunderstood Legacy of Mary Magdalene, the Woman Closest to Jesus.* New York: HarperOne, 2008.

Heineman, Elizabeth D., ed. *Sexual Violence in Conflict Zones: From Ancient World to the Era of Human Rights.* Philadelphia: University of Pennsylvania Press, 2011.

Hunter, Susan Kay. "Prostitution is Cruelty and Abuse to Women And Children." *Michigan Journal of Gender and Law* 1.1 (1993) 91–104.

Ikram, Salima, ed. *Divine Creatures: Animal Mummies in Ancient Egypt.* Cairo: American University Press, 2005.

Kantor, Jodi, and Megan Twohey. "Harvey Weinstein Paid Off Sexual Harassment Accusers for Decades." *New York Times.* October 7, 2017. https://www.nytimes.com/2017/10/05/us/harvey-weinstein-harassment-allegations.html.

Keel, Othmar, and Christoph Uehlinger. *Gods, Goddesses, and Images of God in Ancient Israel.* Minneapolis: Fortress, 1998.

Kippenberg, Juliane. *Soldiers Who Rape, Commanders Who Condone: Sexual Violence and Military Reform in the Democratic Republic of Congo.* New York: Human Rights Watch, 2009.

Kroeger, Catherine Clark, and Mary J. Evans, eds. *The IVP Women's Bible Commentary.* Downers Grove, IL: InterVarsity, 2002.

Maogi, Omega. "Turning Poverty Around." *News 24.* April 4, 2017. https://www.news24.com/SouthAfrica/News/turning-poverty-around-20170403.

Martinez, Florentino Garcia, and Wilfred Watson, trans. *The Dead Sea Scrolls Translated: The Qumran Texts in English.* Leiden: E. L. Brill, 1996.

Masterson, Mark, et al., eds. *Sex in Antiquity: Exploring Gender and Sexuality in the Ancient World.* New York: Routledge, 2015.

Mazar, Amihai. "'The Bull Site,' an Iron Age I Open Cult Place." *BASOR* 247 (1982) 27–42.

————. "A Sacred Tree in the Chalcolithic Shrine at En Gedi." *Bulletin of the Anglo-Israel Archaeological Society* 2 (2000) 31–37.

McKnight, Scot. *The Real Mary: Why Evangelical Christians Can Embrace the Mother of Jesus*. Brewster, MA: Paraclete, 2007.

Menn, Esther Marie. *Judah and Tamar (Genesis 38) in Ancient Jewish Exegesis: Studies in Literary Form and Hermeneutics*. Vol. 51. Supplements to the *Journal for the Study of Judaism*. Leiden: E. J. Brill, 1997.

Miller Bonney, Emily. "Disarming the Snake Goddess: A Reconsideration of the Faience Firurines from the Temple Repositories of Knossos." *Journal of Mediterranean Archaeology* 24.2 (2011) 171–90.

Neusner, Jacob. *Genesis Rabbah: The Judaic Commentary to the Book of Genesis: A New American Translation*. Brown Judaic Studies 104–6. Atlanta: Scholars, 1985.

Newsom, Carol A., et al., eds. *Women's Bible Commentary*. Louisville: Westminster John Knox, 2012.

Ofstad, Harald. *Our Contempt for Weakness: Nazi Norms and Values—and Our Own*. Translated by Clas von Sydow. Gothenburg: Almqvist & Wiksel, 1989.

Park, Andrew Sung, and Susan L. Nelson, eds. *The Other Side of Sin: Woundedness from the Perspective of the Sinned-Against*. Albany, NY: State University of New York Press, 2001.

Perrot, Charles. "The Reading of the Bible in the Ancient Synagogue." In *Mikra: Text, Translation, Reading, & Interpretation of the Hebrew Bible in Ancient Judaism & Early Christianity*, edited by Jan Mulder, 137–59. Peabody, MA.: Hendrickson, 2004.

Ray, J. D. "Animal Cults." In *The Ancient Gods Speak: A Guide to Egyptian Religion*, edited by Donald B. Redford, 86–90. New York: Oxford University Press, 2002.

Renzetti, Claire M., et al., eds. *The Sourcebook on Violence against Women*. Thousand Oaks, CA: Sage, 2001.

Rittner, Carol, and John K. Roth, eds. *Rape: Weapon of War and Genocide*. St. Paul, MN: Paragon, 2012.

Roberts, Yvonne. "India's Daughter." *The Guardian*, February 28, 2015. https://www.theguardian.com/film/2015/mar/01/indias-daughter-documentary-rape-delhi-women-indian-men-attitudes.

Schiffman, Lawrence H. *From Text to Tradition: A History of Second Temple and Rabbinic Judaism*. Hoboken, NJ: Ktav, 1991.

Schmidt, T. C. "Calculating December 25 as the Birth of Jesus in Hippolytus' Canon and Chronicon." *Vigiliae Christianae* 65.5 (2015) 542–63.

Schultz, Celia. "The Romans and Ritual Murder." *Journal of the American Academy of Religion* 78 (2010) 516–41.

Shingal, Ankur. "The Devadasi System: Temple Prostitution in India." *UCLA Women's Law Journal* 22.1 (2015) 107–23.

Smith, Roger W. "Genocide and the Politics of Rape: Historical and Psychological Perspectives." In *Genocide Matters: Ongoing Issues and Emerging Perspectives*, edited by Joyce Apsel and Ernesto Verdeja, 82–105. Abingdon, UK: Routledge, 2013.

Spronk, K. "Rahab." In *Dictionary of Deities and Demons in the Bible*. 2nd extensively rev. ed., edited by Karel van der Toorn et al., 684–86. Leiden: Brill, 1999.

Stiglmayer, Alexandra, ed. *Mass Rape: The War against Women in Bosnia-Herzegovina*. Lincoln: University of Nebraska Press, 1994.

Ussishkin, David. "The Ghassulian Shrine at En Gedi." *Tel Aviv* 7 (1980) 1 44.

Bibliography

van der Toorn, Karel, et al., eds. *Dictionary of Deities and Demons in the Bible.* 2nd extensively rev. ed. Leiden: Brill, 1999.